Pre-Algebra

This book has been correlated to state, national, and Canadian provincial standards. Visit *www.carsondellosa.com* to search for and view its correlations to your standards.

Credits

Author: Theresa Kane McKell

Production: Quack & Company, Inc.

Illustrations: Jeff Van Kanegan

Cover Design: Matthew VanZomeren

Printed in the USA • All rights reserved.   ISBN 0-88724-952-3

Introduction

Pre-Algebra provides students with the conceptual information needed to begin a solid foundation for algebra. It is also to be used as a tool in creating a deeper understanding of the necessary skills required to solve these and future algebraic problems. This book includes a variety of drill and practice problems along with an overview of each skill to be practiced. It is designed to meet the needs of any student at any level of pre-algebra.

The main objective of *Pre-Algebra* is to give students the opportunity to find success in pre-algebraic topics that will eventually lead to success in algebra. To aid in this experience, the book offers an explanation of each skill followed by a variety of activities. These activities will ensure the complete understanding of each skill introduced. Included on page 3 is a "Pre-Algebra Topics and Notes Sheet." This sheet provides students with a place to write facts, figures, and examples for each topic covered. A grid sheet is provided on page 4 which can be copied to complete algebraic graphs.

Pre-Algebra is divided into 11 sections. Each section includes a set of drill and practice student pages, a review of these pages, and a test of the skills learned throughout the section. Each student page consists of a description of the particular skill, several examples, and problems for the students to work to practice learning the skill. Along with the skills the students will learn, they will also get a chance to discover the relationship of mathematical skills to the real world through writing and problem solving.

The concepts covered in this book are relative to any pre-algebra course. The students will develop a conceptual understanding of the pre-algebraic topics and will practice the skills relating to the following concepts: metric system, order of operations, evaluating and simplifying numerical and variable expressions, integer exploration, algebraic properties, fractions and mixed numbers, decimals and estimation, graphing, ratios, proportions, percents, rational numbers, square roots, polynomials, and statistics and probability.

Pre-Algebra is a great way to challenge beginning algebra students and to aid students in need of extra practice. Either focus for using this book will yield the same result—an increased interest and understanding of valuable information needed for present and future mathematics courses. Observe as your students experience how stimulating pre-algebraic topics can really be.

Table of Contents

Pre-Algebra Topics and Notes Sheet

Topic: _____

Notes:

Examples:

Name   Date

Graphs for _____

(title of worksheet)

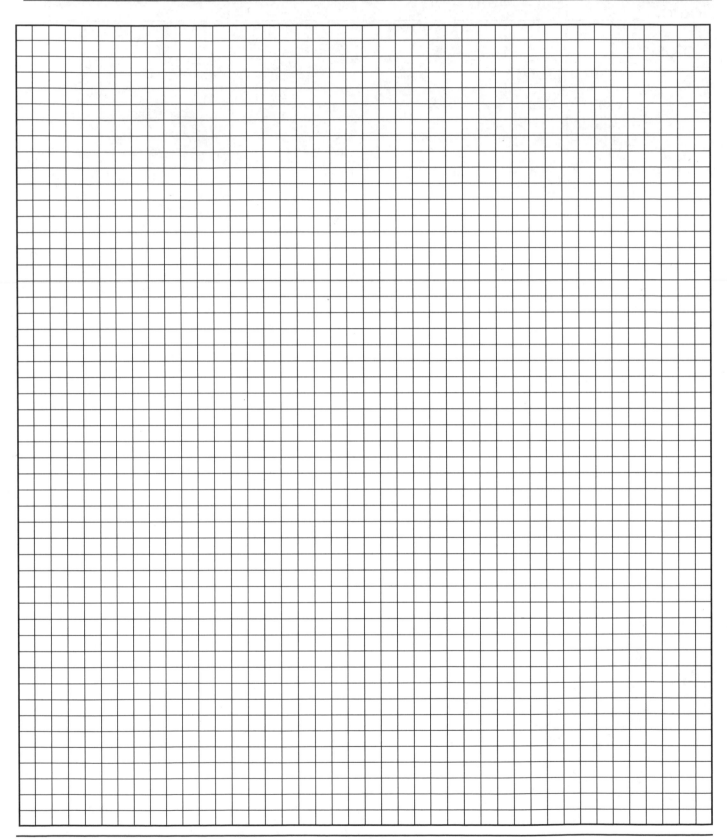

Metric units of measure

Several systems of measurement are used in the world today to describe objects. The one used most is called the metric system. The basic unit of length used in this system is the meter (m). The other metric units of length are named by putting a prefix with the word *meter* as shown in the chart below.

prefix	meaning
kilo	thousand
hecto	hundred
deka	ten
deci	tenth
centi	hundredth
milli	thousandth

1 kilometer (km)	1,000 meters
1 hectometer (hm)	100 meters
1 dekameter (dm)	10 meters
1 meter	10 decimeters (dm)
1 meter	100 centimeters (cm)
1 meter	1,000 millimeters (mm)

Some other common units used in the metric system are the gram (g), which is the basic unit of weight and the liter (L), which is the basic unit of capacity. The prefixes shown in the chart above can also be used in naming the units of weight and capacity.

1 liter= 1,000 milliliters   1 gram = 1,000 milligrams

Answer each question.

1. What does *deka* mean?

2. What does *milli* mean?

3. Which is longer, a centimeter or a meter?

4. Which is heavier, a milligram or a kilogram?

5. Which is more, a centiliter or a liter?

Name the unit each abbreviation represents.

6. km

7. cL

8. g

9. mm

10. kg

11. cm

12. mg

13. kL

Order of operations

A mathematical expression is any combination of numbers using operation symbols such as +, -, x, and ÷. To evaluate an expression, simply find its numerical value. When an expression contains more than one operation, it is important to use the order of operations when finding its value. The rules for the order of operations are as follows:

1. Multiply and divide from left to right.
2. Then add and subtract from left to right.

Find the value of 3 + 2 x 10.

3 + 2 x 10	Multiply.
3 + 20	Add.
23	Final answer.

When there are grouping symbols (parentheses or brackets), simplify within the symbols first and then use the order of operations. Example,

Find the value of 2(8 + 6) - 7 x 3.

2(8 + 6) - 7 x 3	Add.	
2(14) - 7 x 3	Multiply.	2(14) means 2 x 14.
28 - 21	Subtract.	
7	Final answer.	

Name the operation you would do first.

1. 8 + 6 - 3   **2.** 15 ÷ (7 - 2) - 3   **3.** 5 x 4 ÷ 10   **4.** 24 - 21 ÷ 3

Find the value of each expression.

5. 18 - 12 ÷ 4   **6.** 12 - (4 + 7)

7. 7 x (3 + 4)   **8.** 12 ÷ 3 x 2

9. (11 + 4) ÷ 5   **10.** (10 x 4) ÷ (2 x 2)

11. 30 ÷ 6 - 1   **12.** 42 ÷ (5 + 2) x 3

Insert parentheses so each expression has the given value.

13. 56 ÷ 7 x 2; 4   **14.** 12 + 8 ÷ 4; 5

Variables and expressions

An expression that contains a combination of variables, numbers, and at least one operation is called an algebraic expression. A variable is any symbol, such as x, y, or a, that may be replaced with numbers. An algebraic expression can be evaluated by simply replacing the variables in the expression with their assigned values and then finding the numerical value of the expression.

Evaluate each expression if $x = 2$ and $y = 5$.

1. $6x - 2y$ Notice, $6x$ means 6 times x and $2y$ means 2 times y.
   $6(2) - 2(5)$ Replace variables with assigned values. Multiply.
   $12 - 10$ Subtract.
   2 Final answer.

2. $4x + (5 + 3y) - 13$ Remember, evaluate within grouping symbols first.
   $4(2) + (5 + 3(5)) - 13$ Replace variables with assigned values.
   $8 + (5 + 15) - 13$ Multiply.
   $8 + 20 - 13$ Simplify by adding within grouping symbols first. Add.
   $28 - 13$ Subtract.
   15 Final answer.

Evaluate each expression given the value of its variable.

1. $y + 2$; $y = 4$

2. $\frac{6a}{3}$; $a = 3$

3. $\frac{10d}{4} - 8$; $d = 6$

4. $x - 7$; $x = 12$

5. $2c - 4$; $c = 5$

6. $12 - 5z$; $z = 2$

Evaluate each expression if $x = 5$, $y = 2$, and $z = 8$.

7. $2z - 3x$

8. $\frac{6x}{y + z}$

9. $2z - xy$

10. $10x - (4y + z)$

11. $4x - (y + z)$

12. $\frac{7z}{x + y}$

13. $6z + 7y - 3x$

14. $2z + 3x + 4y$

Name _____   Date _____

Symbol translation

Often it is essential to translate words into symbols in order to solve a mathematical problem. Below is a chart with some commonly-used mathematical words and phrases with their possible meanings.

+	−	x	÷
add	subtract	multiply	divide
plus	minus	times	divided by
more than	less than	product of	divided into
sum of	difference	twice	quotient
increased by	decreased by	multiplied by	
added to	subtracted from		

Also, a number can be represented by any variable. It is important to be very careful when arranging the order of terms.

Translate the following phrases into symbols:

1. four more than a number $x + 4$
2. five subtracted from a number $x − 5$
3. subtract a number from nine $9 − x$
4. eight divided by the sum of a number and ten $8 ÷ (x + 10)$

Translate each phrase into an algebraic expression.

1. a number divided by nine

2. five less than a number

3. the sum of a number and ten

4. the product of three and a number

5. twice a number

6. three times a number decreased by two

7. the difference of twelve and a number

8. four more than five times a number

Write a verbal phrase for each algebraic expression.

9. $x + 7$

10. $b ÷ 9$

11. $13 − a$

12. $2(y + 4)$

13. $8n$

14. $4z − 6$

Equations and inequalities

An equation is a sentence that uses an equal sign (=). It is used to show that two expressions have the same value. An inequality is a sentence that uses an inequality sign, such as < or >. These are used to show that two expressions do not have the same value.

    2 < 7 reads: two is less than seven.
    4 + 1 = 5 reads: four plus one equals (is) five.

Note: Both < and > always point to the smaller number. So, any inequality using < or > can be rewritten using the other symbol.

For example, write a sentence using < to show which number is smaller. Then using the same numbers, rewrite the sentence using >.

    1. 4, 8   4 < 8 and 8 > 4
    2. 10 + 2, 13   10 + 2 < 13 and 13 > 10 + 2

1. State the difference between an equation and an inequality.

Rewrite each equation or inequality using words.

2. $14 = 11 + 3$

3. $2 \times 7 < 15$

4. $5x < 30$

5. $12 \div 4 = 3$

6. $x - 3 > 7$

7. $7 = 7$

Write a sentence using < to show which number is smaller. Then rewrite the sentence using >.

8. 9, 12

9. 52, 42 + 8

10. $15 \div 3$, 4

11. 10, 3

12. 8(6), 45

13. 38, 40 − 12

14. 5 + 4, 18

15. 14 − 5, 10

16. 16 + 14, 15 + 18

Variables and equations

Equations that contain variables are open sentences. Open sentences can contain one or more variables and are considered neither true nor false. When a value for the variable(s) can be found making the sentence true, this is called the solution of the equation. The process of finding this solution is called solving the equation. For example, the solution to $8 - 2 = x$ is 6 because 6 makes the sentence true.

Which of the numbers 24, 12, and 6 is the solution of $48 - x = 36$?

Replace x with each of the possible solutions and find which one makes the sentence true.

$48 - 24 = 36$ false $48 - 12 = 36$ true $48 - 6 = 36$ false

Since 12 makes the sentence true, 12 is the solution to the equation.

Solve the equation mentally.

$5x = 30$
$5 \times 6 = 30$ Think: What number times 5 is 30?
$x = 6$

Identify the solution to each equation from the list given.

1. $14 - x = 6$; 4, 6, 8

2. $8 = \frac{z}{7}$; 52, 56, 63

3. $12 = \frac{24}{a}$; 1, 2, 3

4. $100 = 142 - t$; 38, 40, 42

5. $a + 35 = 80$; 35, 40, 45

6. $4x + 1 = 21$; 3, 4, 5

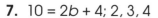

7. $10 = 2b + 4$; 2, 3, 4

8. $6 = 12y - 54$; 3, 4, 5

Identify the solution to each equation.

9. $m + 7 = 10$

10. $48 - t = 0$

11. $\frac{40}{z} = 4$

12. $8x = 72$

13. $138 - y = 8$

14. $16 = 2h$

15. Write two different open sentences that have a solution of 4.

Replacement and solution sets

The set of numbers that can replace a variable in an open sentence is called the replacement set. These numbers can make the sentence either true or false.

The replacement set for the open sentence $x + 8 = 11$ is {1, 2, 3}.

$1 + 8 = 11$	False
$2 + 8 = 11$	False
$3 + 8 = 11$	True

The number 3 is the only number that made the sentence true.

The set of numbers that makes a sentence true is called the solution set. Each number in the solution set is called a solution. Remember, to solve an equation means to find its solution(s). Thus, in the above example, 3 is the solution to $x + 8 = 11$.

Solve $2x > 10$. Use {2, 4, 6, 8}.

$2 \times 2 > 10$	$2 \times 4 > 10$	$2 \times 6 > 10$	$2 \times 8 > 10$
$4 > 10$	$8 > 10$	$12 > 10$	$16 > 10$
False	False	True	True

The solution set is {6, 8}. Thus, 6 and 8 are the solutions to $2x > 10$.

note: If each of the numbers in the replacement set makes the sentence false, there would be no solution in the given replacement set.

Solve each equation using {0, 1, 2, 3} as the replacement set.

1. $x + 7 = 10$

2. $4x + 2 = 10$

3. $7x + 4 = 11$

4. $t + 8 = 8$

5. $3h = 6$

6. $4a \div 2 = 2a$

Solve using the given replacement set.

7. $6(x - 2) = 6x - 12$; {5, 6, 7, 8}

8. $3x > 2x$; {0, 2, 4, 6}

9. $25 - 5y = 15$; {0, 1, 2, 3, 4}

10. $32 = 4a - 8$; {7, 8, 9, 10}

Name _____   Date _____

Formulas

A formula shows the relationship between certain quantities. It is a rule or principle written as a mathematical sentence. For example, the formula to find the distance a car traveled is $d = rt$, where d is the distance, r is the rate, and t is the time.

How far did the car travel in 6 hours at a rate of 55 miles/hour?

$d = rt$	Write the formula.
$d = 55 \times 6$	Substitute the given values. Multiply.
$d = 330$	
330 miles	Answer to the problem (Be sure to include the unit of measure.)

Find the perimeter of a triangle whose sides are $a = 12$ inches, $b = 15$ inches, and $c = 8$ inches. Use the formula: $p = a + b + c$.

$p = a + b + c$	Write the formula.
$p = 12 + 15 + 8$	Substitute the given values. Add.
$p = 35$	
35 inches	Answer to the problem with unit of measure included

Use the formula $d = rt$ to solve each problem for d.

1. $r = 110, t = 3$ **2.** $r = 60, t = 5$ **3.** $r = 75, t = 6$ **4.** $r = 150, t = 12$

Use the given formulas for perimeter to find the perimeter of each geometric figure below.

$p = 2(\ell + w)$ $p = 4s$ $p = 5h$ $p = a + b + c$

5. rectangle; $\ell = 40, w = 15$ **6.** triangle; $a = 8, b = 12, c = 17$

7. regular pentagon; $h = 20$ **8.** square; $s = 18$

9. What is the distance a car traveled driving 65 miles per hour in 8 hours?

10. The sale price of an item is equal to the list price, ℓ, minus the discount, d. Translate this into a formula. Write your own word problem using this formula and solve.

Solving equations using inverse operations

Basics of Algebra

Often equations can be solved using mental math. However, sometimes the solution is not that easy to see. Another way to solve equations is to use inverse operations. Inverse operations have the opposite effect to "undo" what has been done. For example, subtraction would be used to "undo" addition and vice versa. Division is used to "undo" multiplication and vice versa.

Use inverse operations to solve each equation.

1. $x - 10 = 12$
   $x = 12 + 10$ Write the related addition sentence.
   $x = 22$

2. $x + 7 = 21$
   $x = 21 - 7$ Write the related subtraction sentence.
   $x = 14$

3. $8x = 72$
   $x = 72 \div 8$ Write the related division sentence.
   $x = 9$

4. $x \div 10 = 6$
   $x = 6 \times 10$ Write the related multiplication sentence.
   $x = 60$

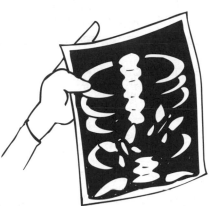

State the inverse of each operation.

1. subtracting 12

2. dividing 7

3. multiplying 4

4. gaining 13 yards

5. adding 21

6. a deposit of $120

Solve each equation using the inverse operation.

7. $7 + n = 30$

8. $144 = 12h$

9. $b - 12 = 21$

10. $96 = c - 6$

11. $9 = \frac{a}{15}$

12. $8y = 96$

13. Write an addition sentence and then write the related subtraction sentence.

14. Write a problem that could be used to solve the equation: $x + \$10 = \$12$. Solve the equation.

Review of Unit 1
Basics of Algebra

Topics covered:

Metric Units of Measure   Variables and Equations
Order of Operations   Replacement and Solution Sets
Variables and Expressions   Formulas
Symbol Translation   Solving Equations using Inverse Operations
Equations and Inequalities

T1. Name the abbreviation for kilometer.

2. What is the difference between the prefixes *centi* and *hecto*?

3. Explain the order of operations you would use to solve $(7 + 2) \div 3 \times 4$. Solve.

Evaluate each expression if $a = 2$, $b = 5$, $c = 10$.

4. $\frac{ab}{c} + 4$ 5. $7b - (2c + a)$

6. Translate "a number multiplied by ten decreased by twelve" into an algebraic expression.

7. Write a verbal phrase describing $3(x + 4)$.

8. Write a sentence using $<$ to show which number is smaller. Then rewrite the sentence using $>$. Use $45 + 10$, 60.

9. If the replacement set is $\{2, 4, 6, 8\}$, identify the solution set for $13 = x + 7$.

10. Write two different open sentences that have a solution of 12.

11. Use $p = 2\ell + 2w$ to find the perimeter of a rectangle whose length (ℓ) is 12 and width (w) is 18.

12. Name the inverse operation that you would use to solve $85 = x + 15$. Solve.

Unit 1 Test

1. Name the most common system of measurement used today.

Give the meaning of each prefix below and give one example using each.

2. kilo   3. centi   4. deka   5. milli

6. Name the order of operations. Solve $16 \div (6 - 2) - 3$ using them.

7. Evaluate $5x - (y + 2z)$ if $x = 6$, $y = 2$, $z = 7$.

8. Write verbal phrases to describe $2x - 7$ and $2x - 7 > 4$.

9. Write a sentence using < to show which number, 35 or $48 - 12$, is smaller. Then rewrite using >.

10. Use mental math to solve $\frac{35}{a} = 7$.

11. Solve $4(x - 3) = 4x - 12$ using the replacement set {0, 1, 2, 3}.

12. What is the distance a car traveled driving 70 miles per hour for 5 hours?

13. Write your own word problem to find the miles per gallon, *mpg*, a car gets given the number of miles driven, *m*, and the number of gallons of gas used, *g*. Use the formula $m \div g = mpg$. Solve your problem to show the solution.

14. State the inverse operation to use to solve $121 = 11h$.

15. Write an addition sentence and then write the related subtraction sentence.

Integers and absolute value

Integers consist of the positive and negative whole values, and the number zero, on a number line. The positive integers are the whole numbers to the right of zero on the number line. The negative integers are the whole numbers to the left of zero. Positive numbers are greater than zero, and negative numbers are less than zero.

     3, 5, 22, and 30 are all positive numbers, and therefore, greater than 0.

     -2, -7, -25, -50 are all negative numbers, and therefore, less than 0.

Integers can be graphed on a number line by locating the integer points. The number that corresponds to a point on a number line is called the coordinate of the point.

To graph a number, find its location on a number line and draw a dot. Place its letter above the dot.

     Name the coordinates of A and B.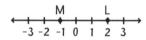
     The coordinate of A is 5.
     The coordinate of B is -3.
     Graph L and M on the number line if L has a
     coordinate of 2 and M has a coordinate of -1.

The absolute value of a number is the distance the number is from zero on a number line. The absolute value of a number is always positive. Therefore, $|5| = 5$ and $|-5| = 5$.

     Simplify $|8| + |-8|$.

          $8 + 8 = 16$ The absolute value of both 8 and -8 is 8. Simply add.

Name the coordinate of each point graphed on the number line.

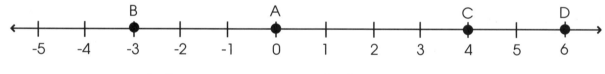

1. A   **2.** B   **3.** C   **4.** D

5. Graph -4, 2, 5, 7 on a number line.

Write an integer for each situation.

6. a deposit of $500   **7.** 10° below zero

8. 4 seconds before takeoff   **9.** a gain of 12 yards

Simplify each.

10. $|-12|$ **11.** $|0|$ **12.** $|-14| - |5|$

13. $-|10|$ **14.** $|-13| + |-12|$ **15.** $-|-15|$

Opposites of whole numbers

A number and its opposite are the same distance from zero on a number line except in the opposite direction. For example, the opposite of 3 is -3 and both are 3 units from zero.

What is the opposite of 0?
   0

Is 0 either positive or negative?
   neither

What is the opposite of -10?
   10

What is the opposite of 12?
   -12

What is the opposite of going up 4 stairs (+4)?
   Going down 4 stairs (-4)

Complete the chart by filling in opposites.

	Activity	Integer	Activity	Integer
1.	300 miles north	300		
2.			up 8 floors	8
3.	10 seconds before liftoff	-10		
4.			$1,500 profit	1,500
5.	12 feet forward			
6.			175 feet above sea level	

Name the opposite of each number.

7. 35

8. -12

9. -70

10. 0

11. 128

12. 52

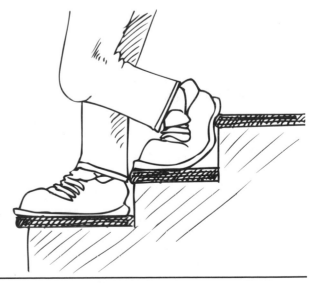

13. Name the integer that is neither positive nor negative and is its own opposite.

Name _____   Date _____

Comparing and ordering

Comparing two numbers often involves inequality symbols. Remember, a mathematical sentence involving these symbols is called an inequality.

Compare -6 and 2 by using two inequalities.

-6 < 2 and 2 > -6   2 is greater than -6 because 2 lies to the right of -6.

$|-6| > |2|$ and $|2| < |-6|$ -6 has the greater absolute value because it lies farther away from zero than 2.

Put the following numbers in order from least to greatest: 33, -2, -10, 43

-10, -2, 33, 43   Notice: -10 is the least value and 43 is the greatest value.

1. List the integers graphed on the number line from least to greatest.

2. Graph -1 and 3 on a number line. Then write two inequalities that show how the integers are related.

Place >, <, or = in each box.

3. 10 ☐ -12

4. |-3| ☐ |3|

5. -11 ☐ -2

6. 0 ☐ |-2|

7. -5 ☐ 0

8. -8 ☐ -14

9. -4 ☐ -6

10. -6 ☐ -4

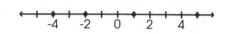

Write an inequality to describe each situation.

11. 4 m is shorter than 6 m.

12. $35 is more than $15.

13. The temperature this morning was 23° F. Now the temperature is 41° F.

Adding integers

Two situations are possible when adding integers: adding integers with same signs and adding integers that have different signs. Remember these two rules when faced with these situations:

1. To add integers that have the same sign, simply add their absolute values. Give the result the same sign as the integers.

   3 + 5
   |3| + |5|
   8   Answer is positive since the integers were both positive.

   -4 + (-7)
   |-4| + |-7|
   4 + 7
   -11   Answer is negative since the integers were both negative.

2. To add integers that have different signs, subtract their absolute values. Give the result the same sign as the integer with the greater absolute value.

   -7 + 5
   |-7| – |5|
   7 – 5   Subtract absolute values.
   -2   Answer is negative because -7 has the greater absolute value.

State whether each sum is **positive**, **negative**, or **zero**.

1. -3 + 5

2. 16 + (-16)

3. 25 + 45

4. -150 + 125

5. 4 + (-11)

6. -11 + (-12)

Find each sum.

7. 17 + (-6)

8. -8 + 3

9. 9 + (-4)

10. -13 + (-10)

11. -12 + (-8)

12. -5 + (-15)

13. Write an addition sentence for the following situation, then solve. Bob made a profit of $4,500 last year and had a loss of $4,800 this year.

Name _____   Date _____

Subtracting integers

Every integer has an opposite. An integer and its opposite are called additive inverses of each other. For example, 3 has an opposite of -3. If 3 and -3 are added together, their sum is 0. The sum of any integer and its opposite will always have a result of 0.

$$3 + (-3) = 0$$
$$-8 + 8 = 0$$

To subtract an integer, simply add its opposite. Thus, change the subtraction problem to an addition problem and solve using the rules already learned for addition of integers.

Subtract 10 − 12

10 + (-12)	Change to addition by adding the opposite of 12.
|-12| − |10|	Subtract absolute values.
12 − 10	
-2	Give result a negative sign since -12 has the greater absolute value.

Subtract 6 − (-13)

6 + 13	Change to addition by adding the opposite of -13.
19	Result is positive since adding numbers with the same positive sign.

Change each problem to an addition problem. Tell whether each answer will be **positive**, **negative**, or **zero**.

1. 1 − 3

2. 10 − (-5)

3. -8 − 14

4. -4 − 7

5. -2 − (-12)

6. 20 − 18

Solve each expression.

7. -10 − 6

8. 12 − (-9)

9. -13 − (-8)

10. 7 − 16

11. 24 − (-26)

12. -5 − 15

13. -40 − 3

14. 23 − 30

15. Explain how the subtraction of integers is related to the addition of integers.

Name _____   Date _____

Multiplying integers

Multiplying integers is just like multiplying positive whole numbers except there is a possibility of negative numbers. Remember the following rules when multiplying integers:

1. The product of two integers with the same sign is positive.

  Multiply 12 x 2

    24   Result is a positive 24 since both integers were positive.

  Multiply -4 • (-9)

    36   Result is a positive 36 since both integers were negative.

2. The product of two integers with different signs is negative.

  Multiply -5 x 7

    -35   Result is a negative 35 since the integers had different signs.

Look at the following example with multiplying 3 integers.

  Multiply -3(-4)(-5)

    12(-5)   Multiply -3 and -4 and the result is a positive 12.

    -60   Result is negative since multiplying integers with different signs.

State whether each product is **positive**, **negative**, or **zero**.

1. 7 x 4

2. -3 x (-5)

3. -7 x 0

4. 6 x (-8)

5. -9 • 9

6. -2 x (-11)

Solve each expression.

7. -10 x 7

8. -16 • (-2)

9. -12 x (-11)

10. -15 x 0

11. 5 x 8

12. 8 x (-10)

13. 6 x (-20)

14. -3 • 13

15. Multiply (-2)(-3)(4). Multiply (-5)(-6)(-1).

Looking at the number of negative signs in both problems, write a rule that will help determine the sign of the product if multiplying two or more integers.

 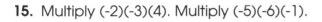

Name _____   Date _____

Dividing integers

When dividing integers, it is important to remember the following rules:

  1. When dividing two integers with the same sign, the quotient is positive.

    Divide $-10 \div (-5)$

        2   Result is a positive 2 since both integers had the same sign.

    Divide $\frac{60}{5}$

        12   Result is a positive 12 since both integers had the same sign.

  2. When dividing two integers with different signs, the quotient is negative.

    Divide $-45 \div 9$

        -5   Result is a negative 5 since integers had different signs.

note: The rules are the same for multiplication of integers as they are for
      the division of integers.

State whether each quotient is **positive**, **negative**, or **zero**.

1. $9 \div 3$

2. $45 \div (-15)$

3. $-28 \div 4$

4. $\frac{0}{-7}$

5. $-16 \div (-8)$

6. $-26 \div (-13)$

Find the value of each expression.

7. $-121 \div (-11)$

8. $\frac{0}{15}$

9. $100 \div (-20)$

10. $\frac{20}{-5}$

11. $-9 \div 3$

12. $\frac{-38}{-19}$

13. $96 \div 16$

14. $\frac{-21}{-7}$

15. Describe a real-life situation in which negative numbers are used. Write your own word
problem involving these negative numbers and division.

Solving addition and subtraction equations

Integer Exploration

To find a solution to an equation, the equation must be solved. To solve addition and subtraction equations you must isolate the variable. Simply subtract if it is an addition problem and add if it is a subtraction problem to get the given variable by itself. Remember the following two properties of equality:

1. If the same number is subtracted from each side of an equation, the two sides remain equal.

   Solve $r + 12 = 67$

   $r + 12 - 12 = 67 - 12$ Subtract 12 from each side of equation.

   $r = 55$ Solve for r.

2. If the same number is added to each side of an equation, the two sides remain equal.

   Solve $x - 16 = 32$

   $x - 16 + 16 = 32 + 16$ Add 16 to each side of equation.

   $x = 48$ Solve for x.

note: It is always a good idea to check each solution by putting it back into the original equation and making sure it creates a true sentence.

State the operation to be used to solve each equation.

1. $x + 7 = 12$

2. $b - 14 = 51$

3. $24 = h + 3$

4. $6 + a = 15$

5. $36 = d - 13$

6. $21 + y = 15$

Solve each equation and check your solution.

7. $n + 10 = 14$

8. $x - 28 = 72$

9. $11 = x - 1$

10. $-600 = c - (-400)$

11. $y - 8 = 8$

12. $64 + h = 36$

13. $-13 = z + 7$

14. $a - 15 = -21$

15. Write an equation whose solution is represented by the number line.

$$\longleftarrow \; | \; | \; | \; \overset{\bullet}{|} \; | \; | \; | \; | \; | \; \longrightarrow$$
$$\qquad -4 \quad -2 \quad 0 \quad 2 \quad 4$$

Solving multiplication and division equations   Integer Exploration

To solve multiplication and division equations, simply divide or multiply on each side of the equation to get the given variable by itself. Remember the following two properties of equality:

1. If you divide each side of an equation by the same nonzero number, the two sides remain equal.

$$\text{Solve} \quad 4x = 84$$

$$\frac{4x}{4} = \frac{84}{4} \qquad \text{Divide each side by 4 to isolate } x.$$

$$x = 21 \qquad \text{Solve for } x.$$

2. If you multiply each side of an equation by the same number, the two sides remain equal.

$$\text{Solve} \quad \frac{x}{21} = 2$$

$$\frac{x}{21} \times 21 = 2 \times 21 \qquad \text{Multiply each side by 21 to isolate } x.$$

$$x = 42 \qquad \text{Solve for } x.$$

note: It is always a good idea to check each solution by putting it back into the original equation and making sure it creates a true sentence.

1. Explain in your own words the steps you would use to solve $\frac{x}{5} = -7$.

2. Write two equations of the forms $ax = b$ and $\frac{x}{b} = a$, each with a solution of 3.

Solve each equation using the inverse operation.

3. $9x = 63$

4. $-96b = 96$

5. $\frac{a}{-6} = 2$

6. $4t = -36$

7. $-64 = -16y$

8. $-25x = -125$

9. $\frac{b}{40} = -3$

10. $\frac{r}{15} = 20$

11. Write a word problem that can be solved using the equation $3x = 21$.

Name _____   Date _____

Solving inequalities by adding and subtracting   **Integer Exploration**

To solve an inequality that involves addition, solve it using subtraction just as you would when solving equations. Likewise, use addition to solve an inequality that involves subtraction. Be sure to always check each solution.

Solve $a + 5 > 11$

$a + 5 - 5 > 11 - 5$ Subtract 5 from each side of the inequality.

$a > 6$ Solve for the variable.

Check: Choose a value greater than 6 and substitute it into the original inequality.

$15 + 5 > 11$

$20 > 11$ True sentence

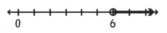

Solve $b - 2 \leq 3$ Note: $\leq$ means less than ($<$) or equal to ($=$).

$b - 2 + 2 \leq 3 + 2$ Add 2 to each side of the inequality.

$b \leq 5$ Solve for the variable.

Check: Choose a value less than or equal to 5 and substitute it into the original inequality.

$4 - 2 \leq 3$

$2 \leq 3$ True sentence

To graph each of these solutions, simply draw a number line and draw a dot on the number found in the solution. The dot will be filled in if the inequality is $\leq$ or $\geq$. The dot will be left unfilled if the inequality is $<$ or $>$. Then simply draw an arrow to the right if it is greater than and to the left if it is less than. See the above graphs.

Write an inequality for each solution set graphed below.

1.

2.

Solve each inequality and check the solution.

3. $x - 7 < 15$ **4.** $-7 + a < 4$ **5.** $r \leq -15 - 9$ **6.** $n - 15 \geq -12$

7. $j + 10 \geq 22$ **8.** $e - 10 > 5$ **9.** $y + 8 > -12$ **10.** $-30 < x - 6$

Write an inequality and graph the solution.

11. Barbara's class can have no more than 30 kids.

12. The Schmidt's house is more than 150 years old.

Name _____   Date _____

Solving inequalities by multiplying and dividing   Integer Exploration

When solving inequalities that involve multiplication or division, it is important to remember the two properties of inequality:

1. When multiplying or dividing each side of an inequality by a positive integer, the inequality symbol stays the same.

    Solve $3x > 30$

        $\frac{3x}{3} > \frac{30}{3}$ Divide each side by 3.

        $x > 10$ Solve for x.

2. When multiplying or dividing each side of an inequality by a negative integer, the inequality symbol must be reversed.

    Solve $\frac{x}{-4} \leq 8$

        $\frac{x}{-4} \cdot -4 \leq 8 \cdot -4$ Multiply each side by -4.

        $x \geq -32$ Solve for x and reverse the inequality symbol since multiplying by a negative number.

note: It is always a good idea to check each solution by putting it back into the original inequality and making sure it creates a true sentence.

1. Write an inequality that can be solved using multiplication where the solution is $x < 12$.

2. Write an inequality that can be solved using division where the solution is $x > 3$.

Solve each inequality and check the solution.

3. $-5y < -35$ 4. $7a \leq -84$ 5. $\frac{m}{3} \leq -10$ 6. $-121 \geq -11z$

7. $\frac{x}{-4} \geq 21$ 8. $-72 > 4b$ 9. $-12t > 108$ 10. $\frac{x}{-2} < -8$

11. The product of an integer and 5 is greater than -32. Find the least integer that makes this true.

12. The quotient of an integer and -3 is less than -18. Find the least integer that makes this true.

Solving equations with two operations

To solve an equation with two operations, work backward and undo each operation one by one. It is important to remember to undo addition and subtraction first, then undo multiplication and division.

Solve $3x + 9 = 21$

           $3x + 9 - 9 = 21 - 9$ Subtract 9 from each side of the equation.

           $\frac{3x}{3} = \frac{12}{3}$ Divide by 3 on each side to isolate the variable.

           $x = 4$ Solve for x.

Check: $3(4) + 9 = 21$

           $12 + 9 = 21$

           $21 = 21$ It is a true sentence. Thus, the solution is 4.

Solve $\frac{x}{5} - 10 = 2$

           $\frac{x}{5} - 10 + 10 = 2 + 10$ Add 10 to each side of equation.

           $\frac{x}{5} \cdot 5 = 12 \cdot 5$ Multiply by 5 on each side of equation.

           $x = 60$ Solve for x.

Check: $\frac{60}{5} - 10 = 2$

           $12 - 10 = 2$

           $2 = 2$ It is a true sentence. Thus, the solution is 60.

note: It is always a good idea to check each solution by putting it back into the original equation and making sure it creates a true sentence.

State the two steps to use to solve each equation.

1. $4x - 8 = 9$ **2.** $\frac{b+7}{4} = 9$ **3.** $52 + \frac{y}{4} = 36$

4. $\frac{a}{2} + 14 = 16$ **5.** $2x + 12 = 18$ **6.** $\frac{z}{5} - 6 = 14$

Solve each inequality and check the solution.

7. $75 + 4x = 3$ **8.** $\frac{z-12}{3} = 4$ **9.** $6 - 3b = 42$ **10.** $\frac{s}{-6} - 9 = 2$

11. $-9 + 2y = 13$ **12.** $\frac{a}{5} - 4 = -6$ **13.** $-7 = -56 + 7t$ **14.** $-18 = \frac{-9+d}{-3}$

15. Write a two-step equation using the numbers 3, 4, and 5, in which the solution is 2.

Review of Unit 2   **Integer Exploration**

Topics covered:

Integers and Absolute Value	Dividing Integers
Opposites of Whole Numbers	Solving Addition and Subtraction Equations
Comparing and Ordering	Solving Multiplication and Division Equations
Adding Integers	Solving Inequalities by Adding and Subtracting
Subtracting Integers	Solving Inequalities by Multiplying and Dividing
Multiplying Integers	Solving Equations with Two Operations

1. Use <, >, or = to make $|-5|$ ☐ $|8|$ a true sentence.

2. Graph 3, 1, 5, -2, -4 on a number line.

3. Give the opposite of -13. Write a real-world situation to represent each of these numbers as opposites.

Simplify each expression.

4. $|-15| - |8|$ **5.** $-12 - 13$ **6.** $40 - 42$ **7.** $\frac{-55}{-11}$

8. $18 + (-21)$ **9.** $-9 - (-16)$ **10.** -15×3 **11.** $120 \div (-12)$

Solve each equation or inequality and check the solution.

12. $x + 5 = 41$ **13.** $-10b = 110$ **14.** $12 + y < 15$ **15.** $-12h \le 72$

16. $-4 + t = 16$ **17.** $\frac{c}{6} = -3$ **18.** $z - 21 \ge -30$ **19.** $\frac{k}{13} > -3$

20. Solve $\frac{-5 + f}{4} = 9$. Explain the step-by-step process you used to solve this problem.

Name _____   Date _____

Unit 2 Test

1. Graph two integers on a number line. Then write two inequalities that show how the integers are related.

2. Write a situation to describe -$1,500.

3. Name the opposite situation of 15 seconds before game time. Give the numbers that represent both situations.

4. Name the integer that is neither positive nor negative. What is its opposite?

Solve each expression.

5. -7 + 17

6. 13 − (-15)

7. 75 • -2

8. -11 − 8

9. $\frac{-39}{3}$

10. (-3)(-2)(-1)(-4)

11. Explain how the subtraction of integers is related to the addition of integers.

Solve each equation.

12. $x + 15 = -9$

13. $\frac{b}{-5} = 15$

14. $\frac{t}{-2} \le 17$

15. $x − 12 < 19$

16. $a − 2 = 6$

17. $-32a = -64$

18. $-7y > 63$

19. $29 \ge z + 11$

20. Write a two-step equation using the numbers 4, 5, and 6, in which the solution is 2. State the steps to solve the equation to get this solution.

Name _____   Date _____

Commutative property

An operation is commutative in mathematics if the order can be changed and the result is still the same. Addition and multiplication both have the commutative property; however, subtraction and division do not. The following states the commutative properties of addition and multiplication:

1. The order in which numbers are added will not change the sum. Thus, for any numbers a and b, $a + b = b + a$.

    $2 + 8 = 8 + 2$ $-9 + 12 = 12 + (-9)$

2. The order in which numbers are multiplied will not change the product. Thus, for any numbers a and b, $a \cdot b = b \cdot a$.

    $9 \cdot 2 = 2 \cdot 9$ $6 \cdot 7 = 7 \cdot 6$

note: These properties are extremely useful when wanting to find a sum or a product quickly using mental computation.

State **yes** or **no** to tell if changing the order of the following activities would change the result.

1. putting your pants on; putting your shirt on

2. washing your hands; washing your face

3. putting a stamp on a letter; writing the letter

4. swimming in a pool; filling the pool with water

5. filling your empty tank with gas; driving on a long trip

Use the commutative property on each equation to make a new equation.

6. $6 + y = 12$ 7. $a + 17 = 21$

8. $x + 4 = 12$ 9. $h \cdot 15 = 75$

10. $56 = t \cdot 7$ 11. $11 + k = 32$

12. $3 = r + 8$ 13. $39 = 13 \cdot f$

Associative property

An operation is associative in mathematics if a set of numbers can be grouped in different ways without changing the result. Addition and multiplication both have the associative property; however, subtraction and division do not. The following states the associative properties of addition and multiplication:

1. The way in which addends are grouped will not change the sum.
   Thus, for any numbers a, b, and c, $(a + b) + c = a + (b + c)$.

   $$(3 + 5) + 7 = 3 + (5 + 7) \qquad (-2 + -7) + 8 = -2 + (-7 + 8)$$

2. The way in which factors are grouped will not change the product.
   Thus, for any numbers a, b, and c, $(a \cdot b) \cdot c = a \cdot (b \cdot c)$.

   $$(12 \cdot 13) \cdot 14 = 12 \cdot (13 \cdot 14) \qquad (-4 \cdot 5) \cdot 9 = -4 \cdot (5 \cdot 9)$$

Use parentheses to group the numbers to make the computation easy.

1. $400 + 60 + 98$ **2.** $3 \cdot 20 \cdot 5$ **3.** $16 \cdot 25 \cdot 4$

4. $2 \cdot 5 \cdot 12$ **5.** $18 + 9 + 91$ **6.** $250 \cdot 4 \cdot 113$

Rewrite each expression using the associative property. Then evaluate the expression.

7. $8 + (2 + 17)$ **8.** $(3 \cdot -4) \cdot 250$ **9.** $68 + (32 + 54)$

10. $(3 \cdot 25) \cdot 4$ **11.** $(21 + 45) + 55$ **12.** $(12 \cdot 5) \cdot 20$

13. $75 + (25 + 19)$ **14.** $-20 \cdot (50 \cdot -29)$ **15.** $5 \cdot (10 \cdot 18)$

16. Show two different ways you can solve the equation $24 = (2x)4$.

17. Show two different ways you can solve the equation $13 + (6 + x) = 20$.

Name _____   Date _____

Zero and one   **Properties Used in Algebra**

Zero and one play important roles in the world of mathematics. The following properties show the relationship between zero and one and the operations of addition and multiplication:

1. Identity Property of Addition: The sum of 0 and any number is that number. Thus, for any number n, $n + 0 = n$.

$$8 + 0 = 8 \qquad\qquad 0 + \text{-}12 = \text{-}12$$

2. Identity Property of Multiplication: The product of 1 and any number is that number. Thus, for any number n, $n \cdot 1 = n$.

$$10 \cdot 1 = 10 \qquad\qquad \text{-}3 \cdot 1 = \text{-}3$$

3. Multiplication Property of Zero: The product of 0 and any number is 0. Thus, for any number n, $n \cdot 0 = 0$.

$$2 \cdot 0 = 0 \qquad\qquad \text{-}5 \cdot 0 = 0$$

note: Any nonzero number divided by itself is one. Zero divided by any nonzero number is zero.

Evaluate each expression.

1. $5 \cdot 1$

2. $0 \cdot 45$

3. $1 \cdot 17$

4. $0 + 185$

5. $32 + 0$

6. $0 \div 57$

Evaluate each expression mentally.

7. $33 + (11 - 11)$

8. $18 - (0 \cdot 52)$

9. $482 \cdot (391 - 390)$

10. $26 \cdot \{9 - (4 + 4)\}$

11. $(24 - 23) \cdot 67$

12. $204 \cdot (19 \cdot 0)$

13. $(43 \cdot 0) \div 1$

14. $(49 - 48) \cdot 411$

15. Write your own statement about multiplying/dividing by 1 and 0.

Distributive property

The distributive property is used quite often in mathematics. It ties addition and multiplication together and is often called the distributive property of multiplication over addition. It states the following:

Distributive Property: For any numbers a, b, and c, $a(b + c) = ab + ac$ and $ab + ac = a(b + c)$.

In other words, the sum of two addends multiplied by a number is the sum of the product of each addend and the number.

1. $3(7 + 2) = 3(7) + 3(2)$ Distribute the 3.
            $= 21 + 6$ Multiply.
            $= 27$ Add to simplify.

2. $3x + x = 24$
    $x(3 + 1) = 24$ Factor out the x.   Note: $x = (1 \cdot x) = 1x$
    $4x = 24$ Add within parentheses.
    $x = 6$ Solve for x to simplify.

3. $17x + 7 + 2x$
    $x(17 + 2) + 7$ Factor out the x to begin simplifying.
    $19x + 7$ Add within parentheses to simplify.

Note: An expression is considered to be in simplest form when it contains no like terms and no parentheses.

State the number to replace the ? in each equation.

1. $4(3 + 7) = (4 \cdot ?) + (4 \cdot 7)$

2. $a + 3a = 1a + 3a = (1 + ?)a$

3. $(10 \cdot 7) + (10 \cdot 6) = 10(7 + ?)$

4. $(6t + 5t) = ?(6 + 5)$

Rewrite each expression using the distributive property. Do not simplify.

5. $4(12 + 15)$

6. $(10 + 13)t$

7. $7r + 8r + 2$

8. $3a + 6b$

9. $x(6 + 8)$

10. $2(5x + 8y)$

Use the distributive property to simplify each expression.

11. $7a + a + 15$

12. $2(b + 4) + 8b$

13. $k + 5 + 7 + 3k$

14. $2c + 6c + 9(c + 3)$

Name _____   Date _____

Factors and divisibility

When two or more numbers are multiplied, each is considered to be a factor of the product.

The factors of 12 are 1, 2, 3, 4, 6, and 12.

A number is divisible by each of its factors. To be divisible, the quotient has to be a whole number and the remainder must be 0.

12 is divisible by 1, 2, 3, 4, 6, and 12 because each quotient would be a whole number and each remainder is 0.

Examples:

1. Is 7 a factor of 63?

$63 \div 7 = 9$ 63 is divisible by 7.
Thus, 7 is a factor of 63.

2. Is 9 a factor of 28?

$28 \div 9 = 3 \text{ R}1$ 28 is not divisible by 9.
Thus, 9 is not a factor of 28.

State the factors of each number.

1. 8   **2.** 18

3. 16   **4.** 24

5. 28   **6.** 35

Write **yes** or **no** to tell whether 4 is a factor of each number.

7. 106   **8.** 1,236   **9.** 144

10. 324   **11.** 906   **12.** 97

Express each number as the product of two factors other than 1.

13. 36   **14.** 45   **15.** 18

16. 54   **17.** 26   **18.** 100

Prime and composite numbers

The mathematical world contains whole numbers that are either prime or composite numbers. A prime number is a whole number that is greater than 1 and has only 1 and itself as factors.

The first ten prime numbers are 2, 3, 5, 7, 11, 13, 17, 19, 23, and 29.

A composite number is a whole number that is greater than 1 and has at least one other factor besides itself and 1. For example, 4 and 15 are composite numbers because they both have more factors besides 1 and themselves.

Each composite number can be expressed as a product of prime numbers through a process called prime factorization.

1. Find the prime factorization of 27.

    $3 \cdot 3 \cdot 3$ Factor 9.
                    Prime factorization

2. Find the prime factorization of 32.

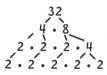

    $2 \cdot 2 \cdot 2 \cdot 2 \cdot 2$ Factor 4 and 8.
                    Factor 4.
                        Prime factorization

Determine whether each number is prime or composite.

1. 45   **2.** 30   **3.** 19   **4.** 33

5. 17   **6.** 29   **7.** 66   **8.** 51

Find the prime factorization of each number.

9. 48   **10.** 27   **11.** 36   **12.** 51

13. 225   **14.** 81   **15.** 144   **16.** 126

17. Explain, in your own words, the difference between a prime and a composite number. Give an example of each.

Name _____   Date _____

Exponents and powers

numbers are often labeled as square numbers. A square number is a number that can be written as the product of two equal factors or as a power.

$16 = 4 \cdot 4$ or 4^2 (4^2 is expressed as 4 to the 2nd power, where 4 is the base, 2 is the exponent, and 4^2 is the power.)

Just as square numbers can be expressed in terms of exponents and powers, many other mathematical situations use them to simplify expressions.

1. Write $a \cdot a \cdot a \cdot a$ using exponents.

   a^4 The exponent is 4 since a is multiplied by itself four times.

2. Express 6^3 as a product of factors and find its value.

   $6 \cdot 6 \cdot 6 = 216$ Multiply 6 by itself 3 times since the exponent is 3.

3. Find the prime factorization of 36. Write the answer using exponents.

   Factor each 6.
   Prime factorization
   2 has an exponent of 2 since 2 is multiplied by itself twice, and
   3 has an exponent of 2 since 3 is multiplied by itself twice.

Write how you read each expression. Name the base and the exponent.

1. 7^2

2. a^8

3. 9^3

4. 3^6

5. 12^4

6. x^5

Rewrite each expression using exponents.

7. $9 \cdot 9 \cdot 9 \cdot 9$

8. $5 \cdot 5 \cdot 5 \cdot 5 \cdot 5 \cdot 5$

9. $b \cdot b \cdot b \cdot b \cdot b \cdot b \cdot b$

10. $a \cdot a \cdot a$

Express the prime factorization of each number using exponents.

11. 75

12. 99

13. 148

14. 54

15. Find the squares of 9 and 10.

Greatest common factors

The greatest common factor (GCF) of two or more numbers is the greatest number that is a factor of each number. Many different methods are used to find the GCF of numbers. For example, one method used is to list the factors of each number and identify the greatest factor common to each number.

Find the GCF of 24 and 72.

Factors of 24: 1, 2, 3, 4, 6, 8, 12, ⃝24
Factors of 72: 1, 2, 3, 4, 6, 8, 9, 12, 18, 24, 36, 72

Thus, the GCF of 24 and 72 is 24. Another method used is to find the prime factorization of each number and then find the product of their common factors.

Find the GCF of 225 and 300.

          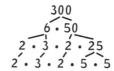   Factor each number to find its prime factorization.

Then find the common factors in these prime factorizations.

$225 = 3 \cdot 3 \cdot 5 \cdot 5$
$300 = 2 \cdot 2 \cdot 3 \cdot 5 \cdot 5$

Thus, the GCF of 225 and 300 is $3 \cdot 5 \cdot 5$ or 75.

1. Explain how to find the GCF of two or more numbers.

2. Name two numbers whose GCF is 12.

Name the GCF of each pair of numbers.

3. $4 = 2^2$
   $16 = 2^4$

4. $12 = 2^2 \cdot 3$
   $20 = 2^2 \cdot 5$

5. $77 = 7 \cdot 11$
   $88 = 2^3 \cdot 11$

6. $9 = 3^2$
   $26 = 2 \cdot 13$

Find the GCF of each set of numbers.

7. 24, 56

8. 32, 128

9. 18, 22, 28

10. 129, 133, 215

11. 25, 85

12. 20, 80, 140

Name _____   Date _____

Least common multiples

A multiple of a number is a product of that number and any whole number.

Multiples of 4: 4, 8, 12, 16, 20, 24, . . .
Multiples of 6: 6, 12, 18, 24, 30, . . .

Notice two of the multiples shared by 4 and 6 are 12 and 24.
These are called common multiples.

The least of the nonzero multiples of two or more numbers that has each given number as a factor is called the least common multiple (LCM) of the numbers. For example, the LCM of 4 and 6 is 12 because 12 is the least multiple common to both numbers. To find the LCM of two or more numbers, find the largest power of each prime factor and multiply these powers.

Find the LCM of 15, 27, and 30.

             Find each prime factorization.

$$15 = 3 \cdot 5$$
$$27 = 3 \cdot 3 \cdot 3 = 3^3$$
$$30 = 2 \cdot 3 \cdot 5$$

Greatest power of 5 is 1.
Greatest power of 3 is 3.
Greatest power of 2 is 1.

Multiply: $2 \cdot 3^3 \cdot 5 = 270$
Thus, the LCM of 15, 27, and 30 is 270.

1. Explain how to find the LCM of two numbers using prime factorizations.

Find the LCM of each pair of numbers.

2. $6 = 2 \cdot 3$
    $10 = 2 \cdot 5$

3. $12 = 2^2 \cdot 3$
    $18 = 2 \cdot 3^2$

4. $25 = 5^2$
    $35 = 5 \cdot 7$

5. $4 = 2^2$
    $15 = 3 \cdot 5$

Find the LCM of each set of numbers.

6. 9, 27   **7.** 30, 50   **8.** 7, 8, 28

9. 12, 30   **10.** 3, 5, 6   **11.** 15, 25, 75

12. Explain how the LCM of a set of numbers can be equal to the greatest number in the set.

Multiplying and dividing monomials

Remember the parts that make up a power. For example, 4^2 is a power, where 4 is the base and 2 is the exponent. In mathematics, powers that have the same base can be multiplied simply by adding their exponents.

$4^5 \cdot 4^3 = 4^{5+3} = 4^8$ The base is 4 and remains unchanged. Add the exponents.

$n^2 \cdot n^7 = n^{2+7} = n^9$ The base is n and remains unchanged. Add the exponents.

Find the product of $(4x^5)(-3x^7)$.

$-12x^{5+7}$ Multiply 4 and –3. The base x remains unchanged.

$= -12x^{12}$ Add the exponents.

Powers that have the same base can also be divided by simply subtracting the exponents.

$\frac{10^4}{10^2} = 10^{4-2} = 10^2$ The base is 10. Subtract exponents.

Divide $\frac{-9ab^7}{3b^5}$

$= -3ab^{7-5}$ Divide –9 and 3.

$= -3ab^2$ Subtract exponents of base b.

---

1. Write a division and a multiplication problem, each with a solution of 5^4.

2. Explain the relationship between multiplying and dividing powers.

Find each product or quotient. Leave each answer in exponential form.

3. $11^6 \cdot 11^7$

4. $b^9 \cdot b^4$

5. $\frac{z^9y^5}{z^3y^3}$

6. $x^3 \cdot x^8$

7. $\frac{3^7}{3^2}$

8. $\frac{-12x^{12}}{3x^7}$

9. $4^5 \cdot 4^2$

10. $\frac{10^{12}}{10^8}$

11. $4c^4d \cdot -5cd^3$

Find each missing exponent.

12. $(6^?)(6^4) = 6^{12}$

13. $\frac{r^?}{r^5} = r^8$

14. $a(a^3)(a^5) = a^?$

15. $\frac{13^7}{13^?} = 1$

Negative exponents

Any negative exponent can be made positive by simply moving the exponent from the numerator to the denominator, or vice versa.

Write each expression using positive exponents.

1. 12^{-4}

   $= \dfrac{1}{12^4}$ Move the base 12 and its exponent to the denominator and the exponent becomes positive.

2. xy^{-5}

   $= \dfrac{x}{y^5}$ Move the base y and its exponent to the denominator. x remains in the numerator because it already has a positive exponent.

Write each expression using negative exponents.

1. $\dfrac{1}{6^8}$

   $= 6^{-8}$ Move the base 6 and its exponent to the numerator.

2. $\dfrac{4}{5^6}$

   $= 4 \cdot 5^{-6}$ Move the base 5 and its exponent to the numerator.

Find the product of $(b^3)(b^{-7})$ and express using positive exponents.

   $(b^3)(b^{-7}) = b^{3 + -7} = b^{-4} = \dfrac{1}{b^4}$ Move b and its negative exponent to the denominator.

Write each expression using positive exponents.

1. 4^{-2} 2. 7^{-3} 3. b^{-12} 4. xy^{-5}

5. x^{-7} 6. 5^{-10} 7. $15^{-4}f^{-1}$ 8. $3(ab)^{-6}$

Write each fraction as an expression using negative exponents.

9. $\dfrac{1}{6^4}$ 10. $\dfrac{1}{18}$ 11. $\dfrac{2}{4^3}$ 12. $\dfrac{c}{d^5}$

13. $\dfrac{1}{b}$ 14. $\dfrac{1}{y^7}$ 15. $\dfrac{x}{y^8}$ 16. $\dfrac{4a}{2b^3}$

Find the product or quotient using positive exponents in the answer.

17. $(a^{-7})(a^3)$ 18. $\dfrac{c^4}{c^5}$

Name _____   Date _____

Review of Unit 3   **Properties Used in Algebra**

Topics covered:

Commutative Property   Exponents and Powers
Associative Property   Greatest Common Factors
Zero and One   Least Common Multiples
Distributive Property   Multiplying and Dividing Monomials
Factors and Divisibility   Negative Exponents
Prime and Composite Numbers

Name the property represented by each statement.

1. $(4 + 6) + 8 = 4 + (6 + 8)$ **2.** $12 \cdot a = a \cdot 12$ **3.** $4 \cdot 1 = 4$

4. $11 + y = y + 11$ **5.** $3(b + 10) = 3(b) + 3(10)$ **6.** $ax + bx = x(a + b)$

7. $9 + 0 = 9$ **8.** $12 \cdot (13 \cdot 20) = (12 \cdot 13) \cdot 20$

9. Name the factors of 48. Express 48 as the product of two of these factors.

10. Identify 92 as a prime or composite number. Give its prime factorization using exponents.

11. Express $12 \cdot 12 \cdot 12 \cdot 12$ using exponents. Name the base and the exponent.

12. Find the GCF of the numbers 18, 36, and 72.

13. Find the LCM of the numbers 4, 8, and 18.

14. Multiply $(b^{10})(b^{-12})(b^2)$. Express answer using positive exponents.

15. Find the quotient of $\frac{ab^7}{a^4b^9}$ using positive exponents. Then write as an expression using negative exponents.

Unit 3 Test

1. Write a mathematical sentence to illustrate each of the following properties: commutative property of addition, commutative property of multiplication, associative property of addition, associative property of multiplication, identity property of addition, identity property of multiplication, multiplication property of zero, and the distributive property.

2. Use the distributive property to simplify $8b + 9b + 24$.

3. Name the factors of 54. Express 54 as a product of two of these factors.

4. What is the difference between a prime and composite number? Give an example of each.

5. Find the prime factorization of 360. Express your answer using exponents.

6. Express $6 \cdot 6 \cdot 6 \cdot 6 \cdot 6$ using exponents. Write how you read this expression. Name its base and the exponent.

7. Find the GCF and LCM of 4, 8, and 20.

8. Explain the difference between finding a GCF and finding an LCM using prime factorizations. Use examples to help with the explanations.

Find each product or quotient. Leave answer in exponential form using positive exponents. Then write expression using negative exponents.

9. $x^{-2} \cdot x^{-5}$

10. $(7^{10})(7^{15})$

11. $(b^8)(b^{-3})(b^{-6})$

12. $\dfrac{c^4 d^7}{c^2 d^9}$

13. $\dfrac{-12a^7}{4a^3}$

14. $\dfrac{4m^{-4}n}{m^{-9}n^3}$

Simplifying fractions

A fraction is considered to be in simplest form, or lowest terms, if its numerator and denominator have no common whole-number factor other than 1.

Simplify $\frac{8}{36}$ to lowest terms.

8 and 36 have a GCF of 4.

$\frac{8 \div 4}{36 \div 4}$ Divide both by the GCF of 4.

$\frac{2}{9}$ Fraction is in simplest form.

Thus, when simplifying fractions, it is important to find the GCF of the numerator and the denominator and divide each by this GCF.

Simplify $\frac{12}{21}$ to lowest terms.

12 and 21 have a GCF of 3.

$\frac{\cancel{12}^{\,4}}{\cancel{21}_{\,7}} = \frac{4}{7}$ An easier way to simplify is to cross out and rewrite numbers after division is completed mentally.

1. What is meant by expressing a fraction in lowest terms? Give an example of a fraction in lowest terms and a fraction that is not.

State the GCF of the numerator and the denominator.

2. $\frac{10}{15}$ 3. $\frac{9}{21}$

4. $\frac{12}{24}$ 5. $\frac{2}{22}$

6. $\frac{30}{51}$ 7. $\frac{33}{77}$

Write each fraction in lowest terms.

8. $\frac{2}{16}$ 9. $\frac{33}{54}$ 10. $\frac{17}{51}$

11. $\frac{18}{45}$ 12. $\frac{25}{40}$ 13. $\frac{18}{108}$

14. $\frac{36}{42}$ 15. $\frac{22}{99}$ 16. $\frac{26}{65}$

Multiplying fractions

To multiply fractions, simply multiply the numerators and multiply the denominators. Thus, the product of any two fractions is equal to the product of their numerators over the product of their denominators. If the fractions have common factors in the numerators and denominators, they can be simplified before they are multiplied.

1. $\frac{1}{4} \times \frac{5}{6}$

$\frac{1 \times 5}{4 \times 6}$ Multiply numerators and multiply denominators.

$\frac{5}{24}$ Final answer in simplest form

2. $\frac{4}{5} \times \frac{7}{12}$

$\frac{1\cancel{4}}{5} \times \frac{7}{\cancel{12}\,3}$ 4 and 12 have a common factor of 4. Divide both by 4.

$\frac{1 \times 7}{5 \times 3}$ Multiply numerators and multiply denominators.

$\frac{7}{15}$ Final answer in simplest form

3. $\frac{9}{21} \times \frac{14}{27}$

$\frac{1\cancel{9}}{3\,\cancel{21}} \times \frac{\cancel{14}\,2}{\cancel{27}\,3}$ 9 and 27 have a common factor of 9. Divide both by 9. 14 and 21 have a common factor of 7. Divide both by 7.

$\frac{1 \times 2}{3 \times 3}$ Multiply numerators and multiply denominators.

$\frac{2}{9}$ Final answer in simplest form

Multiply each expression. Express each answer in lowest terms.

1. $\frac{3}{8} \times \frac{3}{7}$

2. $\frac{3}{10} \times 2$

3. $\frac{1}{12} \times 5$

4. $\frac{2}{5} \times \frac{8}{11}$

5. $\frac{3}{10} \times \frac{2}{13}$

6. $\frac{2}{7} \times \frac{13}{14}$

7. $2 \times \frac{3}{8}$

8. $\frac{1}{2} \times \frac{9}{10}$

9. $\frac{4}{11} \times \frac{3}{4}$

10. $\frac{5}{9} \times \frac{5}{9}$

11. $\frac{3}{5} \times \frac{1}{6}$

12. $\frac{1}{7} \times \frac{1}{6}$

13. Find the product of $\frac{a}{3} \times \frac{4}{5}$.

14. Find $\frac{1}{4}$ of 3 feet.

15. A rope is $\frac{7}{12}$ yards long. How long is $\frac{1}{3}$ of the rope?

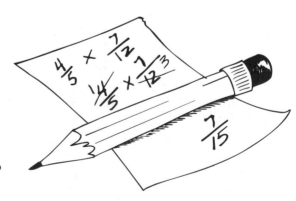

Mixed numbers

A mixed number is the sum of a whole number and a fraction. It is good to use a mixed number when there is an improper fraction. An improper fraction is a fraction whose numerator is larger than its denominator.

$\frac{9}{4}$ is an improper fraction.

To change an improper fraction to a mixed number, following these steps:

1. Divide the numerator by the denominator.

    $9 \div 4 = 2\ R1$

2. Write the whole number answer in step 1 as the whole number and the remainder as the numerator of the fraction with the denominator the same as that in the original improper fraction.

    Thus, the mixed number is $2\frac{1}{4}$.

To change a mixed number to an improper fraction, follow these steps:

Change $3\frac{1}{5}$ to an improper fraction.

1. Multiply the denominator of the fraction times the whole number.

    $3 \times 5 = 15$

2. Add the whole number found in step 1 to the numerator of the fraction in the original mixed number. This is the numerator of the improper fraction.

    $15 + 1 = 16$

3. Write the numerator found in step 2 over the denominator of the original fraction in the mixed number.

    Thus, $\frac{16}{5}$ is the improper fraction.

Express each mixed number as an improper fraction.

1. $3\frac{1}{4}$

2. $6\frac{5}{6}$

3. $2\frac{2}{5}$

4. $1\frac{3}{4}$

5. $4\frac{8}{11}$

6. $5\frac{1}{7}$

7. $8\frac{1}{2}$

8. $5\frac{2}{3}$

Express each improper fraction as a mixed number.

9. $\frac{5}{3}$

10. $\frac{8}{7}$

11. $\frac{17}{7}$

12. $\frac{16}{9}$

13. $\frac{10}{3}$

14. $\frac{26}{5}$

15. $\frac{30}{11}$

16. $\frac{45}{4}$

Multiply. Express answer in lowest terms.

17. $\frac{3}{5} \times \frac{7}{2}$

18. $\frac{5}{4} \times 6$ (Note: first rewrite 6 as $\frac{6}{1}$.)

Multiplying mixed numbers

To multiply mixed numbers, change the numbers to improper fractions.

1. Multiply $2\frac{3}{4}$ x $5\frac{2}{3}$

   $2\frac{3}{4} = \frac{8+3}{4} = \frac{11}{4}$ Change mixed numbers to improper fractions.

   $5\frac{2}{3} = \frac{15+2}{3} = \frac{17}{3}$

   $\frac{11}{4}$ x $\frac{17}{3} = \frac{187}{12}$ Multiply improper fractions.

   $\frac{187}{12} = 15\frac{7}{12}$ Express answer in mixed number form in lowest terms.

2. Multiply $1\frac{1}{2}$ x $\frac{1}{2}$

   $1\frac{1}{2} = \frac{2+1}{2} = \frac{3}{2}$ Change $1\frac{1}{2}$ to a mixed number.

   $\frac{3}{2}$ x $\frac{1}{2} = \frac{3}{4}$ Multiply fractions and express answer in simplest form.

Name the improper fractions that would replace each whole number or mixed number to be able to multiply the expression.

1. 4 x $5\frac{1}{2}$

2. $1\frac{1}{6}$ x $1\frac{1}{7}$

3. 3 x $5\frac{2}{9}$

4. $3\frac{1}{4}$ x $3\frac{1}{5}$

5. 4 x $4\frac{3}{4}$

6. $1\frac{3}{7}$ x $4\frac{1}{10}$

7. $2\frac{1}{2}$ x $2\frac{1}{3}$

8. $6\frac{1}{4}$ •x $7\frac{3}{5}$

9. $3\frac{1}{3}$ x 7

Multiply each expression. Express each answer in lowest terms.

10. $\frac{7}{3}$ x $4\frac{1}{2}$

11. $2\frac{3}{4}$ x $1\frac{1}{2}$

12. $5\frac{1}{5}$ x $3\frac{2}{3}$

13. $\frac{3}{5}$ x 6

14. $8\frac{1}{4}$ x $2\frac{1}{3}$

15. 4 x $5\frac{1}{3}$

Use the formula for the area of a rectangle, $A = \ell \cdot w$, where ℓ is length and w is width, to find the area of each rectangle below.

16. $\ell = 2\frac{1}{2}$ in., $w = 4\frac{1}{4}$ in.

17. $\ell = 8\frac{3}{5}$ ft., $w = 3$ ft.

Dividing fractions and mixed numbers

To divide any two fractions, multiply by the reciprocal of the divisor. Reciprocal numbers are two numbers whose product is 1. To find the reciprocal of a fraction, invert the numerator and denominator.

1. Divide $\frac{3}{2}$ by $\frac{1}{2}$

$\frac{3}{2} \div \frac{1}{2}$ Invert the divisor and change to multiplication.

$= \frac{3}{2} \times \frac{2}{1}$

$= \frac{3 \times 2}{2 \times 1}$ Multiply.

$= \frac{6}{2} = 3$ Simplify the final answer.

2. Divide $2\frac{1}{4}$ by $4\frac{1}{3}$

$2\frac{1}{4} = \frac{9}{4}$ Change mixed numbers to improper fractions.

$4\frac{1}{3} = \frac{13}{3}$

$\frac{9}{4} \div \frac{13}{3}$ Write problem using improper fractions.

$= \frac{9}{4} \times \frac{3}{13}$ Change to multiplication by inverting second fraction.

$= \frac{27}{52}$ Multiply.

1. What are reciprocals? Give an example.

Name the reciprocal of each number.

2. $\frac{4}{7}$ 3. 5   4. $\frac{3}{10}$ 5. $\frac{1}{2}$

Write each division expression as a multiplication expression. Then solve. Write answers in lowest terms.

6. $\frac{1}{4} \div 4$ 7. $1\frac{1}{6} \div 2\frac{1}{2}$ 8. $\frac{1}{5} \div \frac{1}{6}$

9. $\frac{3}{5} \div \frac{7}{10}$ 10. $2\frac{4}{7} \div \frac{1}{3}$ 11. $3\frac{1}{3} \div 5\frac{1}{2}$

Solve each equation for x. Write answers in lowest terms.

12. $6x = 2\frac{1}{2}$ 13. $2x = 3\frac{1}{4}$ 14. $\frac{3}{4}x = 5\frac{1}{2}$

Name _____ Date _____

Adding and subtracting like fractions

To add fractions with like denominators, add the numerators and write the sum over the denominator of the original fractions.

$$\frac{3}{7} + \frac{1}{7}$$

$$\frac{3+1}{7} = \frac{4}{7}$$ Add the numerators. Simplify final answer.

To subtract fractions with like denominators, subtract the numerators and write the difference over the denominator of the original fractions.

$$\frac{8}{9} - \frac{2}{9}$$

$$\frac{8-2}{9} = \frac{6}{9} = \frac{2}{3}$$ Subtract the numerators. Simplify final answer.

To add or subtract mixed numbers, change to improper fractions, add or subtract, and simplify final answer.

$$5\frac{1}{3} + 7\frac{2}{3}$$

$$\frac{16}{3} + \frac{23}{3}$$ Change to improper fractions.

$$\frac{16+23}{3}$$ Add the numerators.

$$\frac{39}{3} = 13$$ Simplify final answer.

Find each sum or difference. Write answers in simplest form.

1. $\frac{3}{5} + \frac{2}{5}$

2. $4\frac{3}{4} - 2\frac{1}{4}$

3. $7\frac{3}{4} - 3\frac{1}{4}$

4. $2\frac{3}{8} + \frac{5}{8}$

5. $2\frac{7}{12} + 6\frac{11}{12}$

6. $5\frac{2}{3} + 1\frac{2}{3}$

7. $11\frac{7}{9} - 2\frac{4}{9}$

8. $2\frac{5}{6} + 9\frac{1}{6}$

9. $13\frac{2}{7} - 9\frac{5}{7}$

Solve each problem.

10. Kim walked $2\frac{1}{4}$ miles. Joe walked $4\frac{3}{4}$ miles. How many more miles did Joe walk than Kim?

11. Jack has a string that is $7\frac{3}{8}$ inches long. He cuts a piece $4\frac{1}{8}$ inches long. How much string does he have left?

         Pre-Algebra

Adding and subtracting unlike fractions

Fractions and Mixed Numbers

To find the sum or difference of unlike fractions, find the least common denominator (LCD) by finding the least common multiple (LCM) of the denominators. Then express each fraction as an equivalent fraction with the least common denominator and add or subtract.

1. Add $\frac{3}{5}$ and $\frac{4}{7}$

   LCM of the denominators is 35. Thus, the LCD is 35.

   $\frac{3}{5} = \frac{?}{35} = \frac{21}{35}$ $35 \div 5 \times 3 = 21$ new numerator
   35 is the LCD.

   $\frac{4}{7} = \frac{?}{35} = \frac{20}{35}$ $35 \div 7 \times 4 = 20$ new numerator
   35 is the LCD.

   $\frac{21}{35} + \frac{20}{35} = \frac{41}{35} = 1\frac{6}{35}$ Add and simplify final answer.

2. Subtract $7\frac{1}{4}$ and $4\frac{1}{3}$

   $7\frac{1}{4} = \frac{29}{4}$ $4\frac{1}{3} = \frac{13}{3}$ Change to improper fractions.
   $\frac{29}{4} - \frac{13}{3}$

   LCM of these denominators is 12. Thus, the LCD is 12.

   $\frac{29}{4} = \frac{?}{12} = \frac{87}{12}$ $12 \div 4 \times 29 = 87$.   new numerator
   12 is the LCD.

   $\frac{13}{3} = \frac{?}{12} = \frac{52}{12}$ $12 \div 3 \times 13 = 52$.   new numerator
   12 is the LCD.

   $\frac{87}{12} - \frac{52}{12} = \frac{35}{12} = 2\frac{11}{12}$ Subtract and simplify answer.

Find the missing number to make an equivalent fraction.

1. $\frac{1}{3} = \frac{?}{24}$ **2.** $\frac{3}{4} = \frac{?}{16}$ **3.** $\frac{2}{3} = \frac{?}{24}$

4. $\frac{1}{5} = \frac{?}{20}$ **5.** $\frac{1}{2} = \frac{?}{40}$ **6.** $\frac{1}{4} = \frac{?}{28}$

Find the LCD of each set of fractions.

7. $\frac{3}{8}, \frac{3}{16}$ **8.** $\frac{7}{10}, \frac{4}{15}$ **9.** $\frac{2}{5}, \frac{1}{6}$ **10.** $\frac{5}{6}, \frac{4}{9}$

Find each sum or difference.

11. $\frac{1}{2} + \frac{3}{4}$ **12.** $\frac{9}{16} - \frac{1}{4}$ **13.** $6\frac{2}{5} + 2\frac{3}{4}$

14. $\frac{5}{6} - \frac{3}{8}$ **15.** $5\frac{2}{7} - 2\frac{3}{8}$ **16.** $4\frac{7}{10} + 9\frac{1}{2}$

Solving equations and inequalities with fractions

Fractions and Mixed Numbers

The same steps taken to solve equations and inequalities involving integers are used to solve equations and inequalities with fractions.

1. Solve $\frac{x}{4} + \frac{1}{2} = \frac{3}{4}$

$\frac{x}{4} + \frac{1}{2} - \frac{1}{2} = \frac{3}{4} - \frac{1}{2}$ Subtract $\frac{1}{2}$ from both sides of the equation.

$\frac{x}{4} = \frac{3}{4} - \frac{2}{4}$ Find the common denominator of the fractions.

$4\left(\frac{x}{4}\right) = \frac{1}{4}(4)$ Multiply by 4 on both sides of the equation.

$x = 1$ Final answer is 1.

2. Solve $3x - 2 \leq \frac{3}{7}$

$3x - 2 + 2 \leq \frac{3}{7} + 2$ Add 2 to both sides of the inequality.

$3x \leq \frac{3}{7} + \frac{14}{7}$ Find the common denominator of the fractions.

$\frac{3x}{3} \leq \frac{17}{7} \div 3$ Divide both sides by 3.

$x \leq \frac{17}{7} \cdot \frac{1}{3}$ Change to a multiplication problem.

$x \leq \frac{17}{21}$ Final answer in lowest terms is $\frac{17}{21}$.

Solve each equation.

1. $\frac{2}{3}x = 5$

2. $\frac{1}{6}x - \frac{2}{7} = \frac{4}{7}$

3. $\frac{x}{2} + 7\frac{1}{2} = 9\frac{1}{2}$

4. $\frac{3}{4}x + 2 = 5\frac{1}{2}$

5. $\frac{4}{5}x = 6\frac{1}{3}$

6. $\frac{7}{8}x - \frac{3}{4} = 6\frac{1}{4}$

Solve each inequality.

7. $\frac{x}{3} < 5$

8. $\frac{3}{2} + \frac{1}{5}x \leq 2\frac{2}{5}$

9. $\frac{4}{5}x > 3\frac{1}{2}$

10. $\frac{x}{2} + \frac{3}{4} \geq \frac{3}{4}$

11. $\frac{3}{8}x - 4 \leq \frac{1}{8}$

12. $\frac{2}{3}x - \frac{1}{6} < 4\frac{2}{3}$

13. State two ways to solve the equation $\frac{2}{3}x = 12$.

14. Write your own equation and inequality using fractions. Explain the steps to use to solve each and solve them.

Review of Unit 4
Fractions and Mixed Numbers

Topics covered:

Simplifying Fractions	Dividing Fractions and Mixed Numbers
Multiplying Fractions	Adding and Subtracting Like Fractions
Mixed Numbers	Adding and Subtracting Unlike Fractions
Multiplying Mixed Numbers	Solving Equations and Inequalities with Fractions

1. Explain what is meant by expressing a fraction in simplest or lowest terms.

2. State the GCF of the numerator and denominator of $\frac{10}{35}$. Simplify the fraction.

3. Find the product of $2 \times \frac{4}{9}$. Explain the steps to do this.

4. Explain what is meant by a mixed number and an improper fraction. Give an example of each.

5. Express the product of $3\frac{3}{4} \times 2\frac{1}{2}$ in lowest terms.

6. Explain the steps to find the quotient of $3\frac{1}{4} \div 6\frac{1}{2}$. Solve.

7. Find the sum of $2\frac{1}{4} + 12\frac{3}{4}$. Find the difference of $12\frac{3}{4} - 2\frac{1}{4}$.

8. Explain how to find the least common denominator (LCD) of a set of unlike fractions.

9. Find the difference of $4\frac{3}{10} - 2\frac{4}{5}$. List the steps you used. What was the LCD?

10. State two ways to solve $\frac{3}{5}x = 9$. Find the answer.

11. Solve $\frac{2}{3}x + 2\frac{1}{2} = 4\frac{3}{4}$.

12. Solve $\frac{1}{4}x - 5\frac{1}{6} \le 3\frac{5}{9}$.

13. Write your own equation or inequality using fractions. Explain the steps used to solve it and solve.

Unit 4 Test

1. State the GCF of 9 and 21. Write these numbers as a fraction in lowest terms using the GCF.

2. Explain how to multiply two fractions. Give an example.

3. Explain how to divide two fractions. Give an example.

4. Explain how to change a mixed number to an improper fraction. Give an example.

Evaluate each expression.

5. $\frac{3}{10} \times \frac{5}{6}$ 6. $4\frac{1}{5} \times 2\frac{2}{3}$ 7. $12 \div 3\frac{6}{7}$ 8. $4\frac{3}{4} \div 2\frac{1}{3}$

9. Solve $\frac{3}{5}x = 6\frac{1}{2}$ for x. State the steps used to solve it.

10. Explain how to add and subtract like fractions. Give an example of each.

11. Explain how to add and subtract unlike fractions. Give an example of each.

State the two steps to use to simplify each expression.

12. $4\frac{3}{8} + 7\frac{3}{8}$ 13. $\frac{3}{5} - \frac{3}{7}$

14. $9\frac{2}{3} - 2\frac{1}{3}$ 15. $7\frac{2}{9} + 8\frac{5}{6}$

16. Explain the steps to solve $\frac{2}{3}x + 4\frac{4}{5} \le 10\frac{3}{10}$ and solve.

17. Write an equation using fractions and state the steps used to solve it. Find the answer.

Decimals as fractions and mixed numbers

Decimals and Estimation

To change a decimal to a fraction, note the place value of the last digit in the number. For example, to change 0.21 (21 hundredths) to a fraction, look at the place value of the 1, since it is the last digit in the number. The 1 is in the hundredths place so 21 would be written over the number 100. Thus, the fraction would be $\frac{21}{100}$.

1. Change 0.324 to a fraction in lowest terms.

$0.324 = \frac{324}{1000} = \frac{81}{250}$

1,000 is the denominator since 4 is in the thousandths place. Simplify.

2. Change 4.25 to a mixed number. (Hint: This will be a mixed number because this is a decimal that is greater than one.)

$4.25 = 4\frac{25}{100} = 4\frac{1}{4}$

The denominator of the fraction is 100 since 5 is in the hundredths place. The whole number is 4. Simplify.

The numbers 10, 100, 1,000, and so on, are called powers of 10, since each can be written using an exponent, (10^1, 10^2, 10^3, and so on). A fraction whose denominator is a power of 10 can very easily be written as a decimal. For example, $\frac{3}{10}$ can be written as 0.3, and $\frac{13}{50}$ can be changed to $\frac{26}{100}$ and written as 0.26.

1. Change $\frac{5}{1000}$ to a decimal.

$\frac{5}{1000} = 0.005$

Two zeros are needed before the 5 so the 5 is in the thousandths place.

2. Change $6\frac{52}{100}$ to a decimal.

$6\frac{52}{100} = 6.52$

Six is the number written before the decimal, and 52 is written to end in the hundredths place.

Write each decimal in word form. Change each decimal to a fraction or mixed number in lowest terms.

1. 0.3

2. 0.05

3. 15.8

4. 5.45

5. 1.47

6. 81.59

7. 0.125

8. 0.455

Express each number as a decimal.

9. $\frac{225}{1000}$

10. $7\frac{9}{100}$

11. $\frac{7}{10}$

12. $\frac{7}{1}$

13. $4\frac{75}{1000}$

14. $41\frac{8}{10}$

Rewrite each fraction with a denominator that is a power of 10. Then rewrite as a decimal.

15. $\frac{3}{5}$

16. $5\frac{11}{50}$

17. $7\frac{29}{500}$

18. $8\frac{17}{20}$

19. $\frac{123}{200}$

20. $10\frac{1}{2}$

Rounding numbers

Decimals and Estimation

When rounding numbers, it is important to remember place values. Look at the chart to the right to help you.

100,000 10,000 1,000 100 10 1 0.10 0.100 0.1000 0.10000 0.100000

Here are the steps to use when rounding numbers.

1. Identify the place value that is going to be rounded.

2. Look at the number to the right of the place value being rounded.

   a. If ≥ 5, replace it and each of the following digits with zeros and increase the place value being rounded by 1.

   b. If < 5, simply replace it and each of the following digits with zeros and stop.

If rounding a place that is to the right of the decimal, drop zeros to the right of this place after you have finished rounding.

1. Round 32,864 to the nearest hundred.

   32,8̲64   First, underline place value to be rounded and
   ▲   then identify number to the right.
   32,400   Since 6 ≥ 5, replace 6 and the digits to its right
                   with zeros and increase 8 by 1.

2. Round 41.782 to the nearest one.

   41̲.782   First, underline place value to be rounded and
   ▲   then identify number to the right.
   42.000   Since 7 ≥ 5, replace the 7 and the digits to the right
                   with zeros and increase 1 by 1.

   42   Drop the zeros to the right of the unit's place unless
                   they are needed as place holders.

Circle the number you would check when rounding to the underlined position. Then round the number.

1. 45,4̲58

2. 7.2̲42

3. 6,1̲25

4. 2,59̲2.29

5. 12.19̲8

6. 23.0̲6

7. 78̲.35

8. 182.61̲68

Complete the chart by rounding as indicated.

number	one	tenth	hundredth	thousandth
9. 685.3714	_____	_____	_____	_____
10. 0.0936	_____	_____	_____	_____
11. 1.4879	_____	_____	_____	_____

Estimating sums and differences

Estimating is a great way to find an answer quickly when a precise answer is not necessary. It also can help you quickly figure out if an answer is reasonable or not.

1. Estimate 29.32 + 41.297 + 11.52

29 + 41 + 12   Estimate each number to the nearest whole number.

= 82   Simply add the estimated numbers.

Thus, 29.32 + 41.297 + 11.52 is about 82.

2. Estimate the difference of 153.789 – 53.182

150 – 50   Estimate each number to the nearest ten.

= 100   Simply subtract the estimated numbers.

Thus, 153.789 – 55.182 is about 100.

note: Round each number to the most convenient place value position. Often the greatest place value position that each of the numbers share is used.

1. Name two examples of numbers that round to a nearest whole number. Show one rounding up and one staying the same.

2. Explain two reasons for using estimation.

Estimate each sum or difference.

3. 13.8 + 49.2

4. 39,415 – 18,918

5. 42 – 39.89

6. 11.25 + 21.92

7. $25 – $19.74

8. 7,604 – 5,142

9. 8.9 + 13.8

10. $9.99 + $4.89

11. 648 – 188

12. 839 + 4,987

13. $315 + $298

14. 77,695 – 42,852

Estimating products and quotients

Decimals and Estimation

When estimating the products and quotients of numbers, it is important to use compatible numbers. Compatible numbers are easy to multiply or divide. These numbers are used to enable mental computation.

1. Estimate 15.52 ÷ 5.72

15 ÷ 5	Estimate numbers to 15 and 5 simply because these numbers are easy to divide mentally.
= 3	Divide.

Thus, 15.52 ÷ 5.72 is about 3.

2. Estimate 15.85 x 9.78

15 x 10	Estimate numbers to 15 and 10 simply because these numbers are easy to multiply.
= 150	Multiply.

Thus, 15.85 x 9.78 is about 150.

Note: Even though some of the numbers above should have been rounded up, it is important to estimate the numbers to create the easiest computation.

1. Give an example of two numbers that are compatible numbers. State why they are compatible.

Estimate each product or quotient.

2. 14.78 x 9.35

3. 109.81 ÷ 8.26

4. 3.91 x 2.04

5. 32,498 x 3.29

6. 21.42 ÷ 6.98

7. 56.319 ÷ 11.46

8. 43.79 ÷ 14.28

9. 122.75 ÷ 7.11

10. 91.65 x 53.42

11. 8.37 x 9.24

12. Is there any way to know if an estimated answer is greater than or less than the actual answer? Explain your answer.

Adding and subtracting decimals

Adding and subtracting decimals is just like adding and subtracting whole numbers except the following rule must be used: The decimal points must be aligned before adding or subtracting.

1. Find the sum of 2.43 + 12.578 + 0.2

$$
\begin{array}{r}
2.43 \\
12.5768 \\
+\ \ 0.2 \\
\hline
15.208
\end{array}
$$

First, align the decimals by writing the numbers vertically.

Then add, aligning the decimal in the answer with the decimals of the numbers added.

2. Find the difference of 1.56 − 0.03

$$
\begin{array}{r}
1.56 \\
-\ 0.03 \\
\hline
1.53
\end{array}
$$

First, align the decimals by writing the numbers vertically.

Then subtract, aligning the decimal in the answer with the decimals of the numbers subtracted.

note: It is sometimes necessary to add zeros to a number to fill in place value positions. For example, 10 − 9.12 would be much easier to compute if zeros were used, making it 10.00 − 9.12. In this case, neither the value of the original problem nor the answer would change.

1. State the rule that must be used when adding and subtracting decimals.

2. Explain the only difference between adding and subtracting decimals and adding and subtracting whole numbers.

Add or subtract each expression.

3. 4.35 + 5.4

4. 52.4 + 0.62 + 2.096

5. 2.55 − 2.05

6. 5.085 − 2.5

7. 16.08 + 3.2

8. 22.3 + 0.89 + 27

9. 12 − 2.73

10. 26.8 − 6.48

Name _____   Date _____

Multiplying decimals   **Decimals and Estimation**

Multiplying decimals is just like multiplying whole numbers. The only difference is the placement of the decimal point in the product. To figure out the placement of the decimal in a product, count the number of digits after each factor's decimal point. Add these numbers together, and this will be the total number of digits after the decimal point in the product.

1. Multiply 23.6 x 13.79

$$
\begin{array}{r}
13.79 \\
\times \quad 23.6 \\
\hline
325.444
\end{array}
$$

   13.79   2 digits after decimal
   x 23.6   1 digit after decimal
   325.444   1 added to 2 gives 3 digits total after the decimal in this product.

2. Multiply 3.12 x 100

   To multiply by a power of 10, simply move the decimal point to the right as many places as there are zeros.

   3.12 = 312   Move decimal 2 places to the right since there are two zeros.

note: When multiplying decimals, estimation is helpful to verify placement of the decimal point in a product.

1. State the rule for placement of the decimal point in a multiplication problem.

To make the statement true, place a decimal point in the factor that is missing a decimal.

2. (82)(.2) = 1.64   **3.** (4.015)(41) = 16.4615

4. (575)(1.2) = 6.900   **5.** (0.6)(216) = 12.96

6. (65.7)(25) = 164.25   **7.** (7.5)(75) = 5.625

Multiply each expression.

8. 7 x 20.2   **9.** 6.2 x 0.35   **10.** 0.2 x 0.18

11. 8.5 x 9.1   **12.** 4.1 x 4.1   **13.** 5.014 x 5.4

14. John bought a case of soda (24 cans) at the store for $0.31 a can. How much money did John spend at the store?

Dividing decimals by whole numbers

Decimals and Estimation

Dividing decimals by whole numbers, is just like dividing whole numbers with one extra step shown below.

1. Divide 5.4 by 9

$$\begin{array}{r} .6 \\ 9\overline{)\,5.4} \\ -\,5\,4 \\ \hline 0 \end{array}$$

= 0.6

Place the decimal point directly above the decimal point in 5.4.
Divide as done with whole numbers.

2. Divide 2.6 by 3

$$\begin{array}{r} .86\overline{6} \\ 3\overline{)\,2.600} \\ -\,2\,4 \\ \hline 20 \\ -\,18 \\ \hline 2 \end{array}$$

= 0.8$\overline{6}$

Place the decimal point directly above the decimal point in 2.6.

Divide as done with whole numbers. Add zeros until you see a pattern.

Use a line above the 6 to show that the 6 repeats.

3. Divide 67.891 by 1,000

To divide numbers by a power of 10, simply move the decimal to the left as many places as there are zeros.

67.891 ÷ 1,000 = 0.067891

Move decimal 3 places to the left since there were 3 zeros. A zero needed to be put in the final answer to hold a place value position.

note: When dividing decimals by whole numbers, sometimes it is necessary to add zeros to a dividend until the remainder is zero or until the answer contains as many digits as one would like or need.

Divide each expression.

1. 0.21 ÷ 6

2. 339.2 ÷ 8

3. 28.35 ÷ 9

4. 9.008 ÷ 4

5. 0.0318 ÷ 6

6. 14.068 ÷ 100

7. 16.8 ÷ 12

8. 6.88 ÷ 16

9. 46.7 ÷ 10

10. If a car uses 16.4 gallons of gas in 4 hours, how many gallons are used per hour?

11. Rob rode his bike 48.3 miles in 3 hours. How many miles did he bike in 1 hour?

Dividing decimals by decimals

To divide by decimals, move the decimals of each number in the problem the same number of places to change the divisor to a whole number. (Just as multiplying the numerator and the denominator of a fraction by the same number gives an equivalent fraction, moving the decimal points in a division problem the same number of places also gives the same answer.)

1. Divide 0.84 by 1.2

$1.2 \overline{)0.84}$

Move the decimals until the divisor is a whole number.

$$12 \overline{)\overset{.7}{8.4}}$$
$$\underline{-84}$$

Divide using the new numbers.

$= 0.7 \quad 0$

Final quotient

2. Divide 0.024 by 0.002

$0.002 \overline{)0.024}$

Move the decimals until the divisor is a whole number.

$$2 \overline{)\overset{12}{24}}$$
$$\underline{-2}$$
$$04$$
$$\underline{-4}$$
$$0$$

Divide using the new numbers.

$= 12$

Final quotient

Change each division problem to make the divisor a whole number.

1. $9.2 \div 1.2$

2. $16 \div 0.48$

3. $0.014 \div 0.005$

4. $10.81 \div 9.1$

5. $0.8 \div 2.6$

6. $24.75 \div 0.95$

Divide each expression.

7. $16.25 \div 0.5$

8. $0.564 \div 1.2$

9. $8.704 \div 3.4$

10. $4.848 \div 0.08$

11. $0.0448 \div 0.014$

12. $10.98 \div 0.02$

13. On Juan's road trip, he spent $15.50 for 12.5 gallons of gas. How much money did he pay per gallon?

Solving equations and inequalities with decimals   Decimals and Estimation

The same skills learned to solve equations and inequalities with integers can be used in solving equations and inequalities with decimals.

1. Solve $\frac{a}{2.2} = 5.1$

   $(2.2)(\frac{a}{2.2}) = 5.1(2.2)$ Multiply both sides by 2.2.

   $a = 11.22$ Solve for a.

2. Solve $0.05x = 9.95$

   $\frac{0.05x}{0.05} = \frac{9.95}{0.05}$ Divide both sides by 0.05.

   $x = 199$ Solve for x.

3. Solve $x + 3.2 = 91.45$

   $x + 3.2 - 3.2 = 91.45 - 3.2$ Subtract 3.2 from both sides.

   $x = 88.25$ Solve for x.

4. Solve $0.2x - 6.8 \leq 7.2$

   $0.2x - 6.8 + 6.8 \leq 7.2 + 6.8$ Add 6.8 to both sides.

   $\frac{0.2x}{0.2} \leq \frac{14}{0.2}$ Divide both sides by 0.2.

   $x \leq 70$ Solve for x.

1. Explain how to solve the equation $0.4x = 6.8$. Then solve.

2. Write an inequality with decimals. State the steps to use to solve it and then solve.

Solve each equation or inequality. Check each solution.

3. $9y \leq 4.5$

4. $0.3d - 7.2 \leq 5.136$

5. $\frac{z}{3.2} = 5.4$

6. $0.6t > 0.96$

7. $7.5a = 2.25$

8. $\frac{z}{4.9} = 9.1$

9. $2b \geq 5.486$

10. $-3.45 + x \geq 10.12$

11. $x + 0.97 = 2.196$

12. $2.4c + 2 = 14.48$

Review of Unit 5

Decimals and Estimation

Topics covered:

Decimals as Fractions and Mixed Numbers	Multiplying Decimals
Rounding Numbers	Dividing Decimals by Whole Numbers
Estimating Sums and Differences	Dividing Decimals by Decimals
Estimating Products and Quotients	Solving Equations and Inequalities with Decimals
Adding and Subtracting Decimals	

1. Explain how to read 2.48. Change this decimal to a mixed number in lowest terms.

2. Rewrite $10\frac{3}{5}$ with a denominator that is a power of 10, and then rewrite as a decimal.

3. Round 351.276 to the nearest hundred and then to the nearest tenth.

Estimate each answer. Tell whether it is a **sum**, **difference**, **product**, or **quotient**.

4. 15.23×9.98
5. $311.02 + 207.56$
6. $61.97 \div 11.24$
7. $\$298 - \$114$

8. Explain the rule that is used when adding and subtracting numbers with decimals.

9. State the rule used to place a decimal point when multiplying.

Evaluate each expression.

10. $7.68 + 12.3$
11. 7.1×0.98
12. 3.1×3.2

13. $28.7 - 5.4$
14. $10.908 \div 9$
15. $0.762 \div 1.2$

16. Explain how to solve $0.2x - 3.5 = 7.1$ and then solve.

17. Solve $\frac{y}{2.3} \leq -5.1$ for y.

Unit 5 Test

1. Rewrite $\frac{4}{25}$ with a denominator that is a power of 10. Then express the fraction as a decimal.

2. Change 7.65 to a mixed number in lowest terms.

3. Name the underlined place value position in 761.4$\underline{5}$8 and round to that place value.

4. Explain two reasons for using estimation.

Estimate each answer by rewriting each expression using estimated numbers.

5. 7.9 + 14.2

6. 24.93 ÷ 5.27

7. 406 + 98 + 822

8. 8,132 − 983

9. 9,451 x 12.95

10. 3,762 ÷ 1,887

11. Write an expression with decimal numbers and explain how to find its sum.

12. Explain the steps used to evaluate 2.196 ÷ 0.3 and evaluate.

Evaluate each expression.

13. 5.49 + 11.206

14. 9.019 x 0.37

15. 6.96 ÷ 8

16. 17 − 2.78

17. 28.94 ÷ 0.004

18. 459.217 x 100

19. Solve 0.4x + 9.2 = 17.128.

20. Write an inequality with decimals. State the steps to use to solve it and then solve.

Ordered pairs and graphing

An ordered pair is a pair of numbers written in a specified order. For example, (3, 2) is an ordered pair. Any ordered pair of numbers can be graphed. For instance, to graph the ordered pair (3, 2), you must move 3 units to the right and then up 2 units.

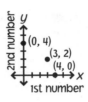

On the same graph, graph the ordered pairs (4, 0) and (0, 4). To graph (4, 0), move 4 units to the right and up 0 units. To graph (0, 4), move 0 units to the right and up 4 units. Graph each of the ordered pairs in the table.

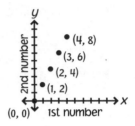

x (1st number)	0	1	2	3	4
y (2nd number)	0	2	4	6	8

note: The x-value is always the first number in the ordered pair and moves to the right and the y-value is the second number in the ordered pair and moves up.

State the moves that would be made to graph each ordered pair.

1. (4, 2)

2. (7, 10)

3. (2, 2)

4. (3, 0)

5. (3, 11)

6. (0, 5)

Name the ordered pair for each point.

7. A

8. B

9. C

10. D

11. E

12. F

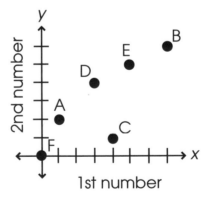

Graph the set of ordered pairs by drawing your own graph.

13. (5, 1), (0, 2), (2, 4), (1, 0), (6, 4), (3, 2)

Integers and the coordinate system

Integers are graphed on a number line. Ordered pairs of integers are graphed on two number lines, called axes. The horizontal number line is called the *x*-axis, and the vertical number line is called the *y*-axis. Look at the coordinate system to the right with important parts labeled.

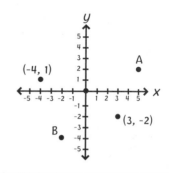

To graph an ordered pair of integers, starting at the origin, move right (*x* is positive) or left (*x* is negative), then up (*y* is positive) or down (*y* is negative). For example, graph (3, -2) and (-4, 1) on the graph below.

The numbers of an ordered pair are called coordinates. To name the coordinates of a point, state the ordered pair of numbers that corresponds to the point. For example, on the graph, find the coordinates of A and B.

The coordinates of A: (5, 2).

The coordinates of B: (-2, -4).

1. Which direction are the positive numbers on the *x*-axis?

2. Which direction are the negative numbers on the *y*-axis?

State the moves that would be made to graph each ordered pair.

3. (3, -2)   **4.** (7, 6)   **5.** (0, -3)

6. (-1, 4)   **7.** (-4, -5)   **8.** (7, 0)

Name the coordinates of each point.

9. A   **10.** B

11. C   **12.** D

13. E   **14.** F

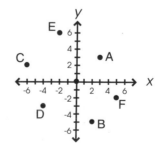

15. On graph paper, draw and label a pair of axes. Then graph each point below, labeling each point with its letter.

A (-1, 5), B (3, -4), C (0, -2), D (6, 3), E (-4, -1), F (-5, 0)

Name _____   Date _____

Graphing linear equations

Remember, to solve an equation means to find a solution that creates a true sentence. The solutions of an equation with two variables are ordered pairs. To find a solution of such an equation, pick any value for x, substitute it into original equation, and solve for the corresponding value of y.

Find three solutions to the equation $y = -3x + 2$.

Choose three values for x.

Use a table to help organize the information.

Do each computation to solve for y.

x	$-3x + 2$	y
-1	$-3(-1) + 2$	5
0	$-3(0) + 2$	2
2	$(-3)(2) + 2$	-4

Thus, the three solutions are (-1, 5), (0, 2), and (2, -4).

Now, graph the equation $y = -3x + 2$.

Use the ordered pairs (points) found in the table and graph each on the coordinate system below.

Draw a line to connect the points.

Notice, if an ordered pair is a solution to an equation of a line, it will be a point on the line.

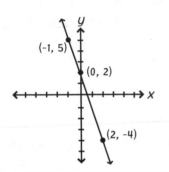

Thus, an equation like $y = -3x + 2$ is a linear equation because its graph is a straight line. An equation like this will have an infinite number of solutions because a line can go in either direction forever.

1. Give a definition of a linear equation.

2. State the steps to use to graph $y = x + 5$.

Find four solutions to each equation. Be sure to write each solution as an ordered pair.

3. $y = 3x$

4. $y = -x$

5. $y - x = 4$

6. $y = 4x + 8$

7. $x + y = 2$

8. $y = x - 5$

On graph paper, graph each equation using a table to find points on the line.

9. $y = x$

10. $y = 2x$

11. $x - y = 5$

12. $y = -x + 2$

13. $x + y = 1$

14. $2x + y = 4$

Slope

The slope m of a line describes how steep it is. The slope is calculated by finding the vertical change (change in y) and the horizontal change (change in x). Thus, the formula for slope is equal to the change in y written over the change in x (slope $m = \dfrac{\text{change in } y}{\text{change in } x}$. The change simply means the difference and can be found by subtracting.

Find the slope of the line that contains the points A(-1, 3) and B(3, 2).

slope = difference in y coordinates / difference in x coordinates

$$m = \frac{2-3}{3-(-1)}$$

$$m = \frac{-1}{4} \qquad m = -\frac{1}{4}$$

Thus, the slope of this line is $-\frac{1}{4}$.

Graph the two points and draw the line.

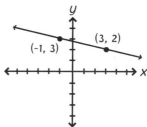

Use the slope to check if the graph is correct by selecting any point on the line and then go down 1 unit and right 4 units. This point should also be on the line.

note: Often the vertical change is referred to as the rise, and the horizontal change is referred to as the run. It is an easy way to remember slope, as the rise over the run.

1. Explain how to find the slope of a line given two points on the line.

2. Explain what is meant when saying a line has a slope of -2.

Find the slope of the line that contains each pair of points.

3. (2, 4), (4, 6)

4. (3, 2), (-2, -8)

5. (-1, 3), (-2, 5)

6. (8, -3), (10, 0)

7. (0, 0), (6, -3)

8. (3, 4), (-1, 4)

9. (-4, 7), (-7, 15)

10. (2, -2), (6, 5)

11. Name two points on a line with a slope of 4. Then graph the line on graph paper.

Intercepts

The x-intercept of a graph is the x-coordinate of the point where the graph crosses the x-axis. The y-intercept of the graph is the y-coordinate of the point where the graph crosses the y-axis. Look at the graph to the right.

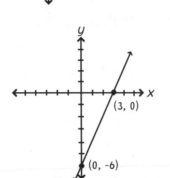

The line crosses the x-axis at the point (4, 0). Thus, the x-intercept is 4. The line crosses the y-axis at the point (0, -2). Thus, the y-intercept is -2.

note: The coordinate of an intercept is always going to be zero.

Another way to graph linear equations is to use the x- and y-intercepts.

Graph $y = 2x - 6$ using the x- and y-intercepts.

To find x-intercept, let $y = 0$.	To find the y-intercept, let $x = 0$.
$0 = 2x - 6$	$y = 2(0) - 6$
$6 = 2x$	$y = 0 - 6$
$3 = x$ (x-intercept is 3)	$y = -6$ (y-intercept is -6)
Thus, the ordered pair is (3, 0).	Thus, the ordered pair is (0, -6).

now, simply graph the intercepts and draw a line that connects them.

1. State the steps to graph a line whose y-intercept is 2 and x-intercept is 4.

2. State the steps to find the x- and y-intercept in the equation $y = 2x - 2$. Solve for the x- and y-intercept.

State the x- and y-intercept for each line.

3. a

4. b

5. c

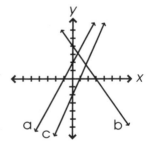

State the x- and y-intercept for each line. Graph each line on graph paper.

6. $-y = x + 4$ 7. $y = 2x + -6$ 8. $y = \frac{1}{4}x + 1$

9. $y = x - 6$ 10. $y = -4x + 8$ 11. $y = \frac{1}{4}x - 2$

Systems of equations

Two equations written together in the same problem are called a system of equations. The solution of a system of equations is the ordered pair that is a solution to both equations. A good method to use to solve systems of equations is to graph the equations on the same coordinate plane. The solution of the system will be the point at which the graphs intersect. For example, solve the system of equations $y = -2x$ and $y = x - 3$ by graphing.

Graph each linear equation. Notice, the lines intersect at the point $(1, -2)$. Thus, the solution of the system of equations is $(1, -2)$.

To check a solution, simply substitute the coordinates into each of the original equations to see if it is a solution to both equations. For example, check the above solution:

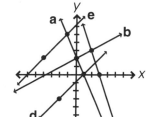

$$y = -2x$$
$$-2 = -2(1)$$
$$-2 = -2 \quad \text{True sentence}$$

$$y = x - 3$$
$$-2 = 1 - 3$$
$$-2 = -2 \quad \text{True sentence}$$

Therefore, this proves $(1, -2)$ is the solution of the system.

Note: When two lines graph into two parallel lines, there is no solution to the system because the lines will never intersect. When two lines graph into the same line, there is infinitely many solutions because any ordered pair on the graph would satisfy both equations.

1. What is meant by a system of equations? Describe its solution.

State the solution of each system of equations by using the graph to the right.

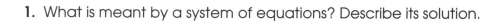

2. a and b

3. a and e

4. a and d

5. b and c

Find the solution of each system of equations by graphing the system.

6. $y = x + 3$
   $y = -x - 5$

7. $y = -x$
   $y = \frac{1}{2}x + 3$

8. $y = -2x$
   $y = 5x$

9. $y = -x + 4$
   $2y = -2x + 8$

10. $y = 3x + 2$
    $y = 3x - 5$

11. $y = 4x - 9$
    $y = 3x - 4$

Graphing inequalities

To graph an inequality, first graph the line it represents. Once the line is graphed, the coordinate plane is divided into two regions. The line is considered the boundary of the two regions. To determine which region represents the solution to the inequality, it is important to test points in either region. The region that contains the point that was a solution to the inequality gets shaded to show all of the solutions.

Graph $y < 4x + 2$.

First, graph the equation $y = 4x + 2$.

A dashed line is drawn since the inequality was $<$ and not $\leq$.

The point $(0, 0)$ is part of the graph since $0 < 4(0) + 2$ is true. Thus, the graph is all points in the region below the boundary. This region is shaded.

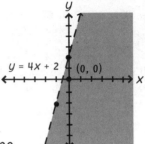

note: If an inequality contains $\leq$ or $\geq$, the graph of the line will be a solid line.
If an inequality contains $<$ or $>$, the graph of the line will be a dashed line.

1. Write an inequality whose graph is all the points above the line $y = 7x + 2$.

2. Explain how to determine which side of the boundary line to shade when graphing an inequality.

State whether the boundary line is dashed or solid.

3. $y \leq 2x - 5$

4. $y > x - 10$

5. $y \geq -4x - 7$

State whether the ordered pair is a solution to the inequality. Write **yes** or **no**.

6. $y > -3x - 2; (1, 4)$

7. $y \geq -x + 4; (5, 0)$

8. $y \leq 4x; (-2, 3)$

9. $4x - 5y < 1; (-1, -1)$

Graph each inequality on graph paper.

10. $y \leq 3$

11. $x + y < 4$

12. $y \leq -x + 5$

13. $x > -2$

14. $x - y \geq 1$

15. $y > 2x - 4$

Name _____   Date _____

Review of Unit 6   **Graphing**

Topics covered:

    Ordered Pairs and Graphing   Intercepts

    Integers and the Coordinate System   Systems of Equations

    Graphing Linear Equations   Graphing Inequalities

    Slope

1. Draw the coordinate system and label the following: *x*-axis, *y*-axis, positive and negative numbers on both axes, and the origin.

State the moves that would be made to graph each ordered pair.

2. (-3, 2)   **3.** (3, 2)   **4.** (-1, -4)   **5.** (1, -4)

Name the coordinates of each point.

6. A   **7.** B

8. C   **9.** D

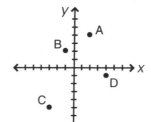

10. On graph paper, graph the equation $y = -3x + 2$ by finding four solutions to the linear equation.

11. Explain how to find the slope of a line that passes through the points (-3, 1), (1, 9). Find the slope.

12. Find the *x*- and *y*-intercept of the line $y = \frac{1}{3}x + 2$. Graph the line on graph paper. Label its *x*-intercept and *y*-intercept points.

13. What is meant by the solution of a system of equations?

14. Find the solution of the following system by graphing on graph paper: $y = 2x + 6$
                                                $y = x + 5$

15. State whether (-2, 4) is a solution to $y < 2x + 1$. Graph the inequality on graph paper.

Name _____   Date _____

1. Which direction are the positive numbers on the x-axis? on the y-axis?

2. On graph paper, draw and label a pair of axes. Then graph the following points, labeling each point with its letter. A (-1, 3), B (-2, -4), C (4, 0), D (-4, 2)

3. State the definition of a linear equation. Give an example.

4. Find four solutions to the equation $y = 2x - 1$. Use these points to graph the line.

5. Find the slope of the line that contains the points (-1, -2), (1, 4).

6. Name two points on a line with a slope of -2. Then graph the line.

7. State the steps to solve for the x- and y-intercept in the equation $y = -\frac{1}{2}x + 3$. Solve for the x- and y-intercept.

8. Use the x-intercept and y-intercept to graph the equation $y = -3x + 6$. Label the intercepts on the graph.

9. What is meant by a system of equations? Describe its solution.

10. Find the solution of the system $y = 4x + 2$ by graphing. Describe its solution.
    $2y = 8x + 4$

11. What kind of lines are needed so there is no solution to a system of equations?

12. Write an inequality whose graph is all the points below the line $y = -2x - 3$.

13. State whether (-5, 1) is a solution to $y > -2x + 6$. Explain why or why not.

14. Graph $y > -x + 4$. State one point that is a solution and one point that is not.

Ratios and rates

A ratio is a comparison by division of two numbers with the same units. Ratios are often expressed as fractions in simplest form or as decimals. A ratio can also be expressed with a colon (1:3, or one to three). For example, express the following as a fraction in simplest form and as a decimal:

3 children out of 9 children have a sibling.

$$\frac{3}{9} = \frac{1}{3}$$ Fraction in simplest form

$$\frac{3}{9} = \frac{1}{3} = 0.3\overline{3}$$ Decimal with a line over the 3 to show repeating

Thus, $\frac{1}{3}$ or $0.3\overline{3}$, of the children have a sibling.

A rate is a comparison of two measurements with different units of measure and is considered to be a special kind of ratio. For example, the ratio of 1 dozen golf balls for $6 can be written: $\frac{1 \text{ doz. golf balls}}{\$6}$. This rate compares golf balls and their price.

To find the price per golf ball, first simplify the rate so the denominator is $1. A rate with a denominator of 1 is called a unit rate.

What is the cost of one golf ball using the above information?

$\frac{1 \text{ doz. golf balls}}{\$6}$ Set up the initial rate.

$\frac{12 \text{ golf balls}}{\$6}$ Simplify 1 doz. = 12 golf balls.

$\frac{12 \div 6}{6 \div 6} = \frac{2}{1}$ To get the unit rate, divide numerator and denominator by 6. Notice 1 is now in the denominator.

$\frac{2 \text{ golf balls}}{\$1}$ Replace in problem adding the units.

Since 2 golf balls cost $1, 1 golf ball costs $.50.

1. What is the difference between a rate and a ratio? Give an example of each.

2. Write a ratio that compares the boys to girls in your class.

Express each ratio or rate as a fraction in simplest form.

3. 12 out of 144

4. 7 out of 9 apples

5. 51 : 17

6. 72 to 9

Express each ratio as a unit rate.

7. 210.8 miles on 12.4 gallons

8. 2.5 in. of rain in 10 hours

9. $10.20 for 15 lbs.

10. $62.50 for 25 tickets

Name _____   Date _____

Equivalent ratios   **Ratios, Proportions, and Percents**

To find equivalent ratios, simply multiply the numerator and the denominator by the same nonzero number.

$\frac{3}{4} = \frac{3 \times 2}{4 \times 2} = \frac{6}{8}$ Find a ratio that is equivalent to $\frac{3}{4}$.

Choose a number to multiply both the numerator and the denominator by. In this case, 2 was chosen.

To change a ratio to lowest terms, or simplified form, simply divide the numerator and the denominator by the same nonzero number.

$\frac{8}{14} = \frac{8 \div 2}{14 \div 2} = \frac{4}{7}$ Change $\frac{8}{14}$ to lowest terms.

The GCF of 8 and 14 is 2 so divide the numerator and the denominator both by 2.

note: To know when a ratio is in its simplest form, look to make sure the numerator and the denominator have no common whole number factors other than 1.

1. Write a ratio of shaded regions to unshaded regions in each rectangle. State if these ratios are equivalent.

  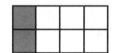 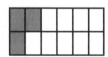

Find two equivalent ratios for each ratio.

2. $\frac{2}{3}$ 3. $\frac{7}{9}$

4. $\frac{1}{8}$ 5. $\frac{13}{20}$

6. $\frac{3}{5}$ 7. $\frac{10}{17}$

Write each ratio in lowest terms.

8. $\frac{2}{10}$ 9. $\frac{14}{56}$

10. $\frac{14}{21}$ 11. $\frac{32}{64}$

12. $\frac{55}{33}$ 13. $\frac{25}{65}$

Name _____   Date _____

Proportions

A proportion is an equation that names two equivalent ratios.

$\frac{3}{4} = \frac{12}{16}$ This is a proportion.

In this proportion, 3 and 16 are called the extremes, and 4 and 12 are called the means. 3×16 and 4×12 are called the cross products. In a proportion, the cross products are always equal, meaning the product of the extremes is equal to the product of the means. For example, $3 \times 16 = 48$ and $4 \times 12 = 48$. This is a great test to show a true proportion. Look at the following examples:

Use cross products to determine if each pair of ratios forms a proportion.

1. $\frac{5}{6}$, $\frac{10}{14}$

   $\frac{5}{6} = \frac{10}{14}$

   $5 \cdot 14 = 6 \cdot 10$

   $70 \neq 60$

   Thus, $\frac{5}{6} \neq \frac{10}{14}$ is not a proportion.

2. $\frac{1}{4}$, $\frac{8}{32}$

   $\frac{1}{4} = \frac{8}{32}$

   $1 \cdot 32 = 4 \cdot 8$

   $32 = 32$

   Thus, $\frac{1}{4} = \frac{8}{32}$ forms a proportion.

Solve the proportion $\frac{n}{3} = \frac{6}{9}$.

$\frac{n}{3} = \frac{6}{9}$

$n \cdot 9 = 3 \cdot 6$ Multiply cross products.

$\frac{9n}{9} = \frac{18}{9}$ Divide both sides by 9.

$n = 2$ Thus, the solution is 2.

---

1. What is the relationship of ratios and proportions? Give an example of a proportion.

2. State the steps to use to solve the proportion $\frac{2}{x} = \frac{20}{30}$ and solve. Identify the means and the extremes.

Use cross products to tell whether each sentence is true. Write **T** (true) or **F** (false).

3. $\frac{3}{2} = \frac{63}{42}$ 4. $\frac{2}{5} = \frac{14}{35}$ 5. $\frac{10}{16} = \frac{5}{9}$ 6. $\frac{7}{5} = \frac{36}{20}$

Solve each proportion.

7. $\frac{3}{4} = \frac{n}{16}$ 8. $\frac{46}{92} = \frac{n}{100}$ 9. $\frac{2}{3} = \frac{24}{n}$ 10. $\frac{n}{2} = \frac{56}{112}$

Set up a proportion to use to solve for each variable and solve.

11. 9 gallons for $27
    x gallons for $9.60

12. 25 candies per 5 boxes
    150 candies per x boxes

Using proportions to solve problems

The most important point to remember when using proportions to help solve problems is to be sure to have the same unit in both numerators, as well as the same unit in both denominators. Once the proportion is set up, simply solve as usual. Look at the following examples:

1. Out of 10 girls, 4 were chosen to go to the state competition. At this rate, how many girls would be chosen out of 50?

   $\frac{4}{10} = \frac{x}{50}$ $\frac{\text{girls in competition}}{\text{total girls}}$ Set up initial proportion. Be sure units match in the numerators and the units match in the denominators.

   $4 \cdot 50 = 10 \cdot x$ Multiply cross products.

   $\frac{200}{10} = \frac{10x}{10}$ Divide both sides by 10.

   $x = 20$ Thus, 20 girls would be chosen out of 50.

2. If a 9-lb. turkey takes 180 minutes to cook, how long would a 6-lb. turkey take to cook?

   $\frac{9}{180} = \frac{6}{x}$ $\frac{lb.}{minutes}$ Set up initial proportion.

   $9 \cdot x = 6 \cdot 180$ Multiply cross products.

   $\frac{9x}{9} = \frac{1080}{9}$ Divide both sides by 9.

   $x = 120$ Thus, it would take a 6-lb. turkey 120 minutes to cook.

Set up a proportion to represent each problem and solve.

1. There are 220 calories in 4 ounces of beef. How many calories are there in 5 ounces?

2. If John can buy 8 liters of soft drinks at the store for $6.40, how much does it cost him to buy 12 liters?

3. Sherri bought a package of pens that contained 15 pens. How many packages should she buy if she needs 240 pens?

4. Steve won his election by a margin of 7 to 2. His opponent had 3,492 votes. How many votes did Steve have?

5. A car traveled 325 miles in 5 hours. How far did the car travel in 9 hours?

6. A recipe asks for 1 ½ cups of chocolate chips for 60 cookies. How many cups would be needed for 36 cookies?

Meaning of percent

Percent is a ratio that compares a number to 100. The symbol for percent is %. For example, $\frac{5}{100}$ is 5% and $\frac{23}{100}$ is 23%. Any percent can be changed to a fraction or a decimal. When percents are changed to fractions, the fractions should be simplified when possible.

1. Change 65% to a fraction and then to a decimal.

$65\% = \frac{65}{100}$ Place 65 over 100. $65\% = 0.65$

$\quad = \frac{13}{20}$ Simplify fraction.   To change to a decimal, simply move decimal two places to the left ($\div 100$).

2. Change 150% to a fraction and then to a decimal.

$150\% = \frac{150}{100}$ Place 150 over 100. $150\% = 1.5$

$\quad = \frac{3}{2} = 1\frac{1}{2}$ Simplify fraction.   Move decimal two places left.

3. Change $62\frac{1}{2}\%$ to a fraction and then to a decimal.

$62\frac{1}{2}\% = \frac{62\frac{1}{2}}{100}$ Place $62\frac{1}{2}$ over 100.

$\quad = 62\frac{1}{2} \div 100$ Divide by 100.

$\quad = \frac{125}{2} \cdot \frac{1}{100}$ Change to multiplication problem.

$\quad = \frac{125}{200} = \frac{5}{8}$ Simplify fraction.

$62\frac{1}{2}\% = 62.5\% = 0.625$ Change $\frac{1}{2}$ to .5 and move decimal two places left.

Write each of the following as a percent.

1. 60 out of 100   2. 55 to 100   3. $\frac{n}{100}$

4. 49 out of 100   5. $\frac{25}{100}$ 6. $\frac{125}{100}$

Change each percent to a fraction in lowest terms and then to a decimal.

7. 5%   8. $28\frac{1}{2}\%$ 9. 8.75%   10. 150%   11. 60%

Complete the table.

percent	fraction	decimal
12. $62\frac{1}{2}\%$		
13. 48%		
14. 0.3%		
15. $\frac{3}{5}\%$		

Changing numbers to percents

To change a decimal to a percent, move the decimal point two places to the right and write the symbol %.

Change 0.765 to a percent.

0.765 = 76.5%   Move decimal two places to the right and write %.

To change a fraction to a percent, set up a percent proportion and then solve, placing the percent symbol after the solution.

Change $\frac{3}{4}$ to a percent.

$\frac{3}{4} = \frac{n}{100}$ Set up percent proportion by setting fraction equal to a number over 100. Solve as a proportion.

$3 \times 100 = 4 \times n$ Multiply cross products.

$\frac{300}{4} = \frac{4n}{4}$ Divide both sides by 4.

$75\% = n$ Solve for unknown and place % after number.

Thus, $\frac{3}{4}$ is equal to 75 percent.

---

1. Describe how to change a decimal to a percent. Give an example.

2. Describe how to change a fraction to a percent. Give an example.

Change each of the following to a percent.

3. 0.32   **4.** 0.125   **5.** $\frac{1}{3}$ **6.** $\frac{4}{25}$

7. 3.5   **8.** 1.475   **9.** $\frac{3}{5}$ **10.** $3\frac{2}{25}$

11. The interest for a home loan is stated as $7.25 per $100. What is the percent of interest?

Change each ratio to a percent.

12. 4 to 2   **13.** $1\frac{1}{2}$ to $1\frac{1}{4}$

14. $\frac{1}{2}$ to $\frac{3}{4}$ **15.** 1.2 : 2.4

16. 5 : 6   **17.** 6 : 4

Three kinds of percent problems

When using proportions to solve percent problems, the denominator of one of the fractions is always going to be 100. Any of the other three numbers can be unknown and asked to be solved. Three problems are presented below in which a different unknown is solved for in each problem.

1. 15 is what percent of 75?

$\frac{15}{75} = \frac{n}{100}$ Identify what is being asked for: the percent. Set up a proportion.

$15 \cdot 100 = 75 \cdot n$ Multiply cross products.

$\frac{1,500}{75} = \frac{75n}{75}$ Divide both sides by 75.

$20 = n$ Solve for the unknown. Thus, 15 is 20% of 75.

2. 9 is 30% of what number?

$\frac{9}{n} = \frac{30}{100}$ Identify what is being asked for: denominator of the fraction.

$9 \cdot 100 = 30 \cdot n$ Multiply cross products.

$\frac{900}{30} = \frac{30n}{30}$ Divide both sides by 30.

$30 = n$ Solve for the unknown. Thus, 9 is 30% of 30.

3. What is 85% of 120?

$\frac{n}{120} = \frac{85}{100}$ Identify what is being asked for: numerator of the fraction.

$\frac{100n}{100} = \frac{85 \times 120}{100}$ Multiply cross products. Divide both sides by 100.

$n = 102$ Solve for the unknown. Thus, 102 is 85% of 120.

note: In example 3, it would be just as easy to change the % to a decimal and multiply by 120, because "of" in mathematics simply means multiply.

Set up a proportion to represent each problem. Solve the proportion.

1. 45 is what percent of 90?

2. What percent of 100 is 19?

3. What is 75% of 60?

4. 35% is 7 out of what?

5. 62% of what number is 9.3?

6. 60% of what number is 50.4?

7. 7 out of 28 is what percent?

8. 90 is 100% of what number?

9. How much is 72% of 54?

10. What percent of 132 is 76.56?

Solving percent word problems

Just as word problems are solved through mathematics, the same methods can be used to solve those problems involving percents.

1. Bob must make at least 75% of his free throws to advance to the final competition. How many free throws must Bob make out of 52 to advance?

   First, identify what you are looking for: # of free throws.

   $\frac{n}{52} = \frac{75}{100}$ Set up a proportion with given information and solve.

   $n \times 100 = 52 \times 75$ Multiply cross products.

   $\frac{100n}{100} = \frac{3,900}{100}$ Divide both sides by 100.

   $n = 39$ Solve for the unknown. Thus, Bob must make 39 free throws.

2. Each item at a sale was reduced 25%. What was the regular price of a shirt that is reduced $9?

   First, identify what you are looking for: item's regular price.

   $\frac{9}{n} = \frac{25}{100}$ Set up a proportion with given information and solve.

   $\frac{900}{25} = \frac{25n}{25}$ Multiply cross products. Divide both sides by 25.

   $36 = n$ Solve for the unknown. Thus, the regular price of the shirt is $36.

Solve each problem by setting up a proportion.

1. Molly made $30 in tips from her customers. If the total of her customers' bills was $200, what percent did her customers tip?

2. How many problems did Robert get right out of 40 if he received an 87.5% on his test?

3. Mary has sold 90 boxes of cookies. If her goal was to sell 120 boxes, what percentage of her goal has she sold?

4. How much did Tom pay in income tax on a gross income of $50,000 if 9% of his income was taxed?

5. How much is a $48 shirt that is on sale for 25% off?

6. Janet borrowed $5,500 from the bank at an interest rate of $7\frac{1}{2}$% for one year. Assuming she pays it back on time, how much interest will she pay?

Name _____   Date _____

Percent of change

The percent of change is the ratio of the amount of change to the original amount. When an amount increases, the percent of change is the percent of increase. When the amount decreases, the percent of change is the percent of decrease, which is negative.

1. Find the percent of change, or the percent of increase, from $150 to $175.

   $175 - 150 = 25$ First, subtract to find the amount of change.

   $25 \div 150 = 0.167$ Divide amount of change by original amount.

   $0.167 = 16.7\%$ Change decimal to a percent.

   Thus, the percent of increase is 16.7%.

2. Find the percent of change, or the percent of decrease, from 145 lbs. to 125 lbs.

   $145 - 125 = 20$ First, subtract to find the amount of change.

   $20 \div 145 = 0.138$ Divide amount of change by original amount.

   $0.138 = 13.8\%$ Change decimal to a percent.

   Thus, the percent of decrease is 13.8%.

State whether each of the following is a percent of increase or a percent of decrease. Then find the actual percent of increase or decrease. Round to the nearest whole percent.

1. before: $24
   after: $20

2. before: 4,985 people
   after: 5,500 people

3. before: 15.6 mL
   after: 20.2 mL

4. before: 190 pounds
   after: 150 pounds

5. before: 130 minutes
   after: 150 minutes

6. before: 92 liters
   after: 110 liters

7. before: $98
   after: $75

8. before: 2,850 points
   after: 1,775 points

9. Explain how to find a percent of change.

10. Most cars depreciate once they've been bought and are driven off a dealer's lot. Mike bought a car in 2000 for $19,500. The value of his car in 2002 was $12,225. What was the percent of decrease of the value of the car?

Name _____   Date _____

Review of Unit 7   **Ratios, Proportions, and Percents**

Topics covered:

Ratios and Rates	Changing Numbers to Percents
Equivalent Ratios	Three Kinds of Percent Problems
Proportions	Solving Percent Word Problems
Using Proportions to Solve Problems	Percent of Change
Meaning of Percent	

1. Explain the difference between a rate and a ratio. Give an example of each.

2. Express the ratio $\frac{32}{68}$ in simplest form.

3. Express the ratio 1,176 miles in 16 hours as a unit rate.

4. Find two equivalent ratios to $\frac{4}{5}$.

5. State the steps used to solve the proportion $\frac{x}{3} = \frac{37}{15}$ and solve. Identify the extremes and the means.

6. Use cross products to tell whether $\frac{3}{5} = \frac{21}{42}$ makes a true sentence. Write **yes** or **no**.

7. A car traveled 288 miles in 4 hours. Set up and solve a proportion to find how far the car traveled in 10 hours.

Write each of the following as a percent.

8. 75 out of 100   9. 0.34   10. $4\frac{5}{25}$ 11. 1.975

12. Change $32\frac{3}{4}$% to a fraction in lowest terms and then to a decimal.

13. What percent is 25 out of 75? Use a proportion to solve.

14. 58% is 34.8 out of what? Use a proportion to solve.

15. If Joe got 70 problems correct and his total percentage was a 93%, how many problems total were there? Round to the nearest whole number.

16. A new bike sells for $98. Two years ago, the bike would have sold for $76. Find the percent of change. State whether it is percent of increase or percent of decrease. Round to the nearest percent.

Unit 7 Test

1. Write the following phrase as a ratio and then express it as a unit rate: $9.45 for 15 lbs.

2. Write $\frac{17}{51}$ in lowest terms and find two more equivalent ratios.

3. Describe the relationship between a ratio and a proportion. Give an example of a proportion.

4. Name the extremes and the means in $\frac{4}{3} = \frac{16}{12}$ and use cross products to tell whether it is a true sentence. Write **yes** or **no**.

5. Solve the proportion $\frac{5}{n} = \frac{25}{75}$ for n.

6. A recipe calls for 4 cups of flour to make 20 pieces of bread. How many cups would it take to make 55 pieces? Use a proportion to solve.

7. Describe how to change a decimal and a fraction to a percent. Give an example of each.

Write each of the following as a percent.

8. 7 out of 100

9. 1.75

10. $\frac{4}{10}$

11. $\frac{25}{75}$

12. 1 : 5

13. $\frac{1}{4}$

14. Change 32% to a fraction in lowest terms and then to a decimal.

15. 19.2 is what percent of 30?

16. How much is 45% of 52?

17. John borrowed $12,000 from the bank at an interest rate of $6\frac{1}{2}$% for one year. Assuming he pays it back on time, use a proportion to find how much interest he will pay.

18. Write your own percent of change problem. State whether it is a percent of increase or a percent of decrease and solve. Round answer to the nearest whole percent.

Comparing rational numbers

A rational number is any number that can be named by a fraction with a numerator and a denominator that are integers. For example, $-\frac{1}{2}$, $4\frac{3}{4}$, and -3.25 are each rational numbers because $-\frac{1}{2} = \frac{-1}{2}$, $4\frac{3}{4} = \frac{19}{4}$, and $-3.25 = -3\frac{1}{4} = -\frac{13}{4} = \frac{-13}{4}$.

To compare two rational numbers, simply rewrite each so that they have the same positive denominator and then compare the numerators.

Compare $-\frac{8}{9}$ and $\frac{1}{3}$.

$-\frac{8}{9} = \frac{-8}{9}$

$\frac{3}{4} = \frac{3}{9}$ Change to the same denominator.

$-8 < 3$ Compare the numerators.

So $\frac{-8}{9} < \frac{3}{9}$ and $-\frac{8}{9} < \frac{1}{3}$.

If two fractions have the same positive denominator, the fraction with the greater numerator is the greater number.

Compare $-\frac{5}{7}$ and $-\frac{6}{7}$.

$-5 > -6$

So $-\frac{5}{7} > -\frac{6}{7}$.

Circle the fraction that is greater in each set.

1. $\frac{6}{13}$ or $\frac{8}{13}$

2. $-\frac{1}{3}$ or $\frac{1}{3}$

3. $-\frac{2}{9}$ or $-\frac{7}{9}$

4. $-\frac{9}{20}$ or $-\frac{13}{20}$

5. $\frac{5}{12}$ or $-\frac{11}{12}$

6. $-\frac{1}{3}$ or $\frac{3}{4}$

Write <, >, or = in each ☐ to make a true sentence.

7. $\frac{7}{10}$ ☐ $\frac{3}{10}$

8. $\frac{5}{16}$ ☐ $\frac{3}{4}$

9. $\frac{1}{2}$ ☐ $\frac{1}{4}$

10. $-\frac{7}{8}$ ☐ $-\frac{8}{9}$

11. $-\frac{11}{24}$ ☐ $-\frac{5}{8}$

12. $\frac{7}{5}$ ☐ $\frac{6}{4}$

13. $-\frac{8}{12}$ ☐ $-\frac{4}{6}$

14. $-\frac{3}{4}$ ☐ $-\frac{9}{12}$

15. $\frac{2}{3}$ ☐ $-\frac{3}{4}$

16. $-\frac{7}{4}$ ☐ $-\frac{5}{3}$

Adding and subtracting with rational numbers

To add and subtract with rational numbers, use the same steps as with whole numbers, remembering the rules for addition and subtraction of negative numbers.

1. Add $-0.35 + (-2.5)$

$$\begin{array}{r} -0.35 \\ + -2.5 \\ \hline -2.85 \end{array}$$

First, line up the decimal points.

Apply the correct sign to each number.

Add, giving the answer a negative sign since both numbers are negative.

2. Subtract $-\frac{1}{2} - \frac{3}{4}$

$-\frac{1}{2} = -\frac{2}{4}$ and $\frac{3}{4} = \frac{3}{4}$ First, find a common denominator.

$-\frac{2}{4} - \frac{3}{4} = \frac{-2 - 3}{4}$ Subtract the numerators.

$= -\frac{5}{4} = -1\frac{1}{4}$ Simplify with the correct sign.

3. Add $2\frac{3}{4} + (-4\frac{1}{8})$

$2\frac{3}{4} = \frac{11}{4}$ and $-4\frac{1}{8} = -\frac{33}{8}$ First, change to improper fractions.

$\frac{11}{4} = \frac{22}{8}$ Find a common denominator.

$\frac{22}{8} + -\frac{33}{8} = \frac{22 + -33}{8}$ Add the numerators.

$= -\frac{11}{8} = -1\frac{3}{8}$ Simplify with the correct sign.

State whether each sum is **positive**, **negative**, or **zero**.

1. $-2.7 + 3.2$

2. $-\frac{1}{2} + \frac{3}{4}$

3. $-0.86 - (-4.5)$

4. $4\frac{1}{8} - 6\frac{1}{7}$

5. $\frac{3}{4} - \frac{4}{5}$

6. $-2\frac{2}{3} + 2\frac{4}{6}$

Find each sum or difference.

7. $-4.2 - 3.7$

8. $3\frac{1}{2} - (-5\frac{1}{4})$

9. $\frac{3}{8} \quad \frac{1}{2}$

10. $8.4 - 9.6$

11. $-0.68 + 1.29$

12. $-\frac{7}{8} + (-\frac{3}{4})$

13. $-7\frac{1}{2} - 3\frac{1}{4}$

14. $-9\frac{3}{4} + 3\frac{1}{4}$

15. Use the formula, $p = w + m$, to find the retail price (p) if the markup (m) on a CD is $3.59 and the wholesale price (w) is $12.97.

Name _____   Date _____

Solving equations with rational numbers   **Rational Numbers**

To solve equations with rational numbers, solve for the variable by adding or subtracting, remembering rules for addition and subtraction of negative numbers.

1. Solve $x + 9.25 = -7.82$

$x + 9.25 - 9.25 = -7.82 - 9.25$ Subtract 9.25 from both sides.

$x = -7.82 + (-9.25)$ Change to an addition problem.

$x = -17.07$ Solve for x.

2. Solve $3\frac{1}{4} + x = 2\frac{1}{2}$

$3\frac{1}{4} - 3\frac{1}{4} + x = 2\frac{1}{2} - 3\frac{1}{4}$ Subtract $3\frac{1}{4}$ from both sides.

$x = \frac{5}{2} - \frac{13}{4}$ Change to improper fractions.

$x = \frac{10}{4} - \frac{13}{4}$ Find a common denominator.

$x = \frac{10 - 13}{4}$ Subtract the numerators.

$x = \frac{10 + (-13)}{4}$ Change to an addition problem.

$x = -\frac{3}{4}$ Solve for x.

Solve each equation for x.

1. $x - 4.3 = -6.4$

2. $x + 10\frac{3}{5} = -4\frac{1}{15}$

3. $x + 7.5 = -10.2$

4. $-\frac{1}{8} + x = \frac{5}{16}$

5. $x - (-\frac{1}{4}) = -\frac{3}{8}$

6. $x + 2\frac{3}{7} = 1\frac{3}{14}$

7. $x + \frac{2}{5} = -\frac{3}{10}$

8. $-5.7 + x = -4.8$

9. $x - 8\frac{2}{3} = -10\frac{3}{6}$

10. $-\frac{4}{9} + x = -\frac{1}{3}$

11. Explain what is meant by a rational number. Give two examples.

12. Write your own equation involving a variable and rational numbers. Explain the steps to use to solve the equation and solve.

Multiplying and dividing with rational numbers

To multiply or divide rational numbers using decimals, multiply or divide and then find the sign of the product. Remember, same signs give a positive product and different signs give a negative product.

Multiply 2.2×-3.1
$2.2 \times -3.1 = -6.82$

Different signs gives a negative product.

Divide $19 \div 0.25$

$$0.25 \overline{)19.00} = 76$$
$$\underline{-\ 175}$$
$$150$$
$$\underline{-\ 150}$$
$$0$$

Since same signs, a positive 76 is the solution.

To multiply or divide rational numbers using fractions, multiply or divide and then find the sign of the product.

Multiply $\frac{5}{8} \times \frac{-2}{3}$

$\frac{5}{8} \times \frac{-2}{3} =$

$= \frac{-10}{24}$

$= \frac{-5}{12}$

Divide $\frac{-7}{9} \div \frac{-4}{5}$

$\frac{-7}{9} \times \frac{-5}{4} =$

$= \frac{35}{36}$

To multiply or divide rational numbers using mixed numbers, multiply or divide and then find the sign of the product.

Multiply $-3\frac{4}{5} \times 2\frac{1}{3}$

$-\frac{19}{5} \times \frac{7}{3} =$

$= \frac{133}{15}$

$= -8\frac{13}{15}$

Divide $-4\frac{1}{5} \div -3\frac{1}{2}$

$\frac{-21}{5} \div \frac{-7}{2} =$

$\frac{-21}{5} \times \frac{-2}{7} =$

$= \frac{42}{35}$

$1\frac{7}{35} = 1\frac{1}{5}$

State whether each product or quotient is **positive** or **negative**.

1. 12.5×5.8

2. $\frac{4}{9} \div -\frac{3}{10}$

3. $-3\frac{1}{7} \div 10\frac{4}{5}$

4. $-3\frac{1}{5} \times -7\frac{3}{8}$

5. $-0.74 \div -0.17$

6. $\frac{3}{14} \times -\frac{2}{7}$

Find each product or quotient.

7. 1.8×-4.5

8. $-9\frac{1}{2} \times 3\frac{1}{5}$

9. $-\frac{5}{6} \div -\frac{7}{8}$

10. $-\frac{4}{5} \times -\frac{9}{10}$

11. 1.782×-2

12. $-4\frac{2}{7} \div -3\frac{3}{14}$

13. Find the value of $(-10.2 + 1.5) \div -0.5$.

14. Find the value of $(-3.7 - 9.1) \times 4.6$.

Name _____   Date _____

Reciprocals

Reciprocals are two numbers whose product is 1. To find the reciprocal of a fraction, simply flip the fraction.

$$\frac{4}{7} \times \frac{7}{4} = 1 \qquad\qquad \frac{2}{9} \times \frac{9}{2} = 1$$

The reciprocal of a negative number is always negative.

$$-\frac{3}{4} \times -\frac{4}{3} = 1 \qquad\qquad -\frac{9}{7} \times -\frac{7}{9} = 1$$

To find the reciprocal of an integer or a mixed number, first change the number to a fraction and then flip the fraction.

$$7 = \frac{7}{1} \qquad\qquad\qquad -4\frac{1}{3} = -\frac{13}{4}$$

$$\frac{7}{1} \times \frac{1}{7} = 1 \qquad\qquad -\frac{13}{3} \times -\frac{3}{13} = 1$$

Note: It is important to see that 0 has no reciprocal.

$$\frac{0}{1} \times \frac{1}{0} \neq 1 \qquad$$ We cannot write this because a number can never be divided by zero. Therefore, 0 has no reciprocal.

1. Explain how to find the reciprocal of a number.

2. Name the number that has no reciprocal and explain why it cannot have a reciprocal.

3. What positive or negative numbers are equal to their own reciprocals?

Name the reciprocal.

4. $\frac{1}{3}$ **5.** $-\frac{4}{1}$

6. -18   **7.** $-6\frac{3}{10}$

8. $-12\frac{1}{2}$ **9.** -1

10. $\frac{5}{16}$ **11.** $5\frac{1}{2}$

Name each reciprocal in decimal form. (Hint: First change each decimal to a fraction.)

12. 0.5   **13.** 2.5   **14.** 1.6   **15.** 0.08

Solving rational equations with multiplication and division

To solve an equation involving decimals, multiply or divide, remembering to watch the signs, and solve for the variable.

Solve $-3.2x = 6.4$

$\dfrac{-3.2x}{-3.2} = \dfrac{6.4}{-3.2}$ Divide both sides by -3.2.

$x = -2$ Solve for x.

To solve an equation involving mixed numbers or fractions, multiply or divide, remembering to watch the signs, and solve for the variable.

Solve $-\dfrac{3}{4}x = -4\dfrac{1}{3}$

$-\dfrac{4}{3}\left(-\dfrac{3}{4}x\right) = \left(-4\dfrac{1}{3}\right)\left(-\dfrac{4}{3}\right)$ Multiply both sides by $-\dfrac{4}{3}$.

$x = -\dfrac{13}{3}\left(-\dfrac{4}{3}\right)$ Change the mixed number to an improper fraction.

$x = \dfrac{52}{9} = 5\dfrac{7}{9}$ Multiply and then simplify.

note: Multiplying by the reciprocal is the same as dividing by the number.

Solve each equation for x.

1. $5.2x = -34.84$

2. $-4\dfrac{1}{2}x = 3$

3. $\dfrac{x}{-3.1} = 4.5$

4. $5\dfrac{2}{3}x = -51$

5. $-2.7x = -7.29$

6. $\dfrac{x}{-3} = \dfrac{2}{5}$

7. $\dfrac{2}{5}x = -\dfrac{2}{3}$

8. $-4.2x = 25.2$

9. $14 = -\dfrac{2}{3}x$

10. $-\dfrac{7}{3}x = -\dfrac{7}{10}$

Remember to watch the signs!

11. Write an equation with fractions. State the steps to use to solve and then solve.

12. A number is divided by -2.3, and the result is -8.5. Write the equation and solve for the number.

Rational equations with two operations

To solve rational equations with two operations, perform the operations to solve for the variable, remembering the addition, subtraction, multiplication, and division rules for negative numbers.

1. Solve $-\frac{1}{2}x - 0.72 = -2.74$

     $-\frac{1}{2}x - 0.72 + 0.72 = -2.74 + 0.72$ Add 0.72 to both sides of the equation.

     $-\frac{1}{2}x = -2.02$ Add unlike signs.

     $-2(-\frac{1}{2}x) = -2.02(-2)$ Multiply both sides by –2.

     $x = 4.04$ Solve for x.

2. Solve $\frac{5}{6}x - \frac{2}{3} = -\frac{1}{4}$

     $\frac{5}{6}x - \frac{2}{3} + \frac{2}{3} = -\frac{1}{4} + \frac{2}{3}$ Add $\frac{2}{3}$ to both sides of the equation.

     $\frac{5}{6}x = -\frac{1}{9} + \frac{6}{9}$ Find a common denominator.

     $\frac{5}{6}x = \frac{5}{9}$ Add.

     $(\frac{6}{5})(\frac{5}{6}x) = \frac{5}{9}(\frac{6}{5})$ Multiply $\frac{6}{5}$ by both sides of the equation.

     $x = \frac{30}{45} = \frac{2}{3}$ Solve for x. Simplify.

Solve each equation for x.

1. $-3 = \frac{1}{4}x + 5$

2. $\frac{x}{9.1} + 4 = -1.4$

3. $-4x - \frac{3}{4} = \frac{3}{8}$

4. $7x - \frac{2}{15} = -\frac{5}{6}$

5. $\frac{5}{6}x + \frac{1}{6} = -\frac{2}{3}$

6. $\frac{x}{-5} - 2.5 = 3.2$

7. $-3.2x - 0.4 = 5.8$

8. $-\frac{7}{2}x + \frac{5}{4} = \frac{31}{8}$

9. State the steps you would use to solve $\frac{2}{3}x - 4 = -\frac{1}{2}$ and then solve for x.

10. Write your own two-step equation. State the steps you would use to solve it and solve for the variable.

Mean, median, and mode   **Rational Numbers**

The mean of a set of data is the average, meaning the sum of the data divided by the number of pieces of data.

     Using the data below, find the mean.

        9, 15, 18, 4, 21, 11, 6

        $9 + 15 + 18 + 4 + 21 + 11 + 6 = 84$ Add.

        $84 \div 7 = 12$ Divide by the number of data.

     Thus, the mean is 12.

The median of a set of data is the number in the middle when the data is arranged in order.

     Using the above data, find the median.

        4, 6, 9, 11, 15, 18, 21   Arrange in order from least to greatest.

     Thus, 11 is the median because it is the middle number.

note: When there are two middle numbers, find their mean, or average.

The mode of a set of data is the number or item that appears the most often in the set. For example, in the above set of data, there is no mode because no one item appears more than the other. Look at the example below.

        3, 2, 3, 4, 2, 3,

The mode of this set of data would be 3 since it appears three times, more than any of the other numbers.

1. Explain mean, median, and mode. Give an example of each by writing a set of data with at least six numbers.

List the data in each set from least to greatest. Then find the mean and median. Round to the nearest tenth when necessary.

2. 6, 8, 3, 11, 9, 37, 21   3. 23, 64, 52, 25, 40, 46, 9, 29, 31

4. 12, 46, 58, 14, 49, 9, 16, 25   5. 3.7, 7.1, 9.0, 5.7, 4.2

6. 101, 132, 151, 91, 85   7. 0.5, 1.7, 0.6, 9.2, 0.9, 0.2

8. Write a set of data with a mean of 9.

9. What is the mode in the following set of data?

     2, 3, 2, 6, 4, 3, 4, 2, 6, 4, 2

Scientific notation

A number is expressed in scientific notation if it is written as a number between 1 and 10 multiplied by a power of 10. For example, 3.2×10 is written in scientific notation.

1. Write 350,000 in scientific notation.

   3.5×10^5 Write as a number between 1 and 10 by moving the decimal five places to the left. Multiply by 10^5.

2. Write -0.0000012 in scientific notation.

   -1.2×10^{-6} Write as a number between 1 and 10 with the negative sign by moving the decimal six places to the right. Multiply by 10^{-6}.

note: When changing a large positive or negative number to scientific notation, the power of 10 is positive. When changing a small positive or negative number to scientific notation, the power of 10 is negative.

A number not written in scientific notation is written in standard form. For example, 25,000 is written in standard form. To change a number from scientific notation to standard form, move the decimal to the right if the power of 10 is positive and to the left if the power of 10 is negative.

1. Write -4.1×10^4 in standard form.

   -41,000   Move the decimal four places to the right since the power of 10 is a positive 4.

2. Write 5.2×10^{-2} in standard form.

   0.052   Move the decimal two places to the left since the power of 10 is negative 2.

1. Explain how to write each of the following numbers in scientific notation: 254,000 and 0.000053.

Write each number in scientific notation.

2. 6,784,000

3. -0.0000045

4. 0.0089

5. 90,000,000

6. -273,000

7. 0.0000000000017

Write each number in standard form.

8. -3.2×10^7

9. 5.05×10^3

10. 7.6×10^5

11. -8.003×10^{-4}

12. 2.389×10^{-6}

13. -4.32×10^{-9}

Review of Unit 8
Rational Numbers

Topics covered:

Comparing Rational Numbers
Adding and Subtracting with Rational Numbers
Solving Equations with Rational Numbers
Multiplying and Dividing with Rational Numbers
Reciprocals

Solving Rational Equations with
Multiplication and Division
Rational Equations with Two Operations
Mean, Median, and Mode
Scientific Notation

1. State which fraction is greater: $-\frac{9}{7}$ or $-\frac{13}{14}$.

2. When two fractions have the same positive denominator, how do you know which is greater?

3. Find the sum and difference of these numbers: -3.41 and 2.56.

4. Find the product and quotient of these numbers: -7.04 and 3.2.

5. Give a definition of reciprocals and give one example.

6. Name the reciprocal of 0.02 in standard form.

Solve each equation for x.

7. $x - 5.2 = -7.2$

8. $-\frac{x}{5.2} = 3.2$

9. $\frac{x}{6} + 5.6 = -2.6$

10. $x - (-\frac{1}{3}) = -\frac{5}{6}$

11. $-\frac{3}{4}x = -\frac{2}{9}$

12. $-6x - \frac{5}{12} = \frac{7}{12}$

13. $x + (-9\frac{1}{2}) = 11\frac{1}{4}$

14. $-4.5x = 27.9$

15. $-\frac{x}{3} - 1\frac{2}{3} = -5\frac{1}{3}$

16. Write a set of data with a mean of 8 and a median of 15.

17. What is the mode of the following set of data? 3, 4, 2, 5, 3, 3

18. Write 7,640,000 in scientific notation.

19. Write 9.06×10^{-8} in standard form.

Unit 8 Test

1. Give a definition of a rational number. Give an example.

2. State which fraction is greater: $-\frac{3}{5}$, $-\frac{2}{3}$.

3. Find the sum of $-\frac{3}{8}$ and $\frac{1}{4}$.

4. Find the difference of $-4\frac{1}{2}$ and $-9\frac{3}{4}$.

5. Solve $x - \frac{4}{5} = -\frac{9}{10}$ for x.

6. Find the product of 13.2 and -3.1.

7. Find the quotient of $-4\frac{5}{6} \div -6\frac{5}{12}$.

8. Evaluate $(12.4 - 16.2) \times 2.9$.

9. Explain how to find the reciprocal of a number. Give an example.

10. What is the only number that does not have a reciprocal? Explain.

11. Solve $-\frac{4}{7}x = -\frac{9}{10}$.

12. State the steps used to solve $-\frac{x}{3.9} + 4.2 = 1.7$. Solve.

13. Explain what is meant by the mean, median, and mode of a set of data. Give an example of each of by writing your own set of data with at least seven numbers.

14. Explain how to write -0.000000415 in scientific notation and write it in that form.

15. Explain how to write 7.98×10^6 in standard form and write it in that form.

Square roots

Every positive number has two square roots. The square root of a number is one of its two equal factors. For example, 49 has two square roots, 7 and -7, because $7 \times 7 = 49$ and $-7 \times -7 = 49$. The symbol, $\sqrt{}$, called a radical sign, is used to indicate a nonnegative square root, while $-\sqrt{}$ is used to indicate a negative square root.

1. Find two solutions for $x = 25$
   Since $5 \times 5 = 25$ and $-5 \times -5 = 25$, the solutions are 5 and -5.

2. Find $\sqrt{81}$
   $\sqrt{81} = 9$

3. Find $-\sqrt{100}$
   $-\sqrt{100} = -10$

note: Zero has only 1 square root $\sqrt{0} = 0$.

1. Explain the square root of a number. Give an example.

Find two solutions for each equation.

2. $a^2 = 4$ **3.** $w^2 = 64$ **4.** $x^2 = 9$ **5.** $z^2 = 49$

6. $c^2 = 1$ **7.** $n^2 = 100$ **8.** $y^2 = 144$ **9.** $b^2 = 400$

Find each square root.

10. $\sqrt{25}$ **11.** $-\sqrt{225}$

12. $-\sqrt{81}$ **13.** $\sqrt{49}$

14. $-\sqrt{36}$ **15.** $-\sqrt{196}$

16. $\sqrt{121}$ **17.** $\sqrt{289}$

18. Evaluate $\sqrt{169} - (-\sqrt{81})$.

Approximate square roots

Numbers like 16, 25, 36, and 49 are called perfect squares because when the square root is taken of each of these numbers, the answer is a whole number. If a number is not a perfect square, it is important to see that estimation can be used. For example, 56 is not a perfect square, but it is greater than 49 (7^2) and less than 64 (8^2). So, it is easy to see the square root of 56 should be greater than 7 and less than 8 as shown below.

$$\sqrt{49} < \sqrt{56} < \sqrt{64}$$

$$7 < \sqrt{56} < 8$$

Since 56 is closer to 49 than 64, the best whole number estimate for $\sqrt{56}$ would be 7.

Look at another example.

Estimate $-\sqrt{13}$

9 and 16 are the closest perfect squares to 13.

$$-\sqrt{16} < -\sqrt{13} < -\sqrt{9}$$

$$-4 < -\sqrt{13} < -3$$

Since 13 is closer to 16 than 9, the best integer estimate is -4.

Find the best integer estimate for each square root.

1. $\sqrt{91}$

2. $\sqrt{83}$

3. $-\sqrt{67}$

4. $\sqrt{650}$

5. $-\sqrt{150}$

6. $-\sqrt{240}$

7. $\sqrt{7.85}$

8. $-\sqrt{96}$

9. $-\sqrt{115}$

10. $\sqrt{200}$

11. Is it possible to find the square root of a negative number? Explain why or why not.

12. Is it possible for a to be a negative number in the equation $a^2 = b$? Explain why or why not.

Square roots and rational numbers

Rational numbers have square roots, just as whole numbers do. To find the square root of a rational number, simply find the square root of the numerator and then the square root of the denominator.

1. Find $\sqrt{\frac{9}{16}}$

   $\dfrac{\sqrt{9}}{\sqrt{16}}$ Write as square root of numerator and square root of denominator.

   $= \dfrac{3}{4}$ Find each square root and write as a fraction.

2. Find $\sqrt{0.49}$

   $\sqrt{0.49} = \sqrt{\frac{49}{100}}$ Write the decimal as a fraction.

   $\dfrac{\sqrt{49}}{\sqrt{100}}$ Write as square root of numerator and square root of denominator.

   $= \dfrac{7}{10} = 0.7$ Find each square root and write as a fraction and simplify into a decimal.

1. How do you find the square root of a fraction? Give an example.

Find each square root as a fraction. Simplify.

2. $\sqrt{\dfrac{9}{25}}$

3. $-\sqrt{\dfrac{16}{36}}$

4. $\sqrt{\dfrac{64}{144}}$

5. $\sqrt{\dfrac{169}{225}}$

6. $\sqrt{\dfrac{1}{4}}$

7. $-\sqrt{\dfrac{49}{121}}$

8. $-\sqrt{\dfrac{81}{100}}$

9. $-\sqrt{\dfrac{25}{49}}$

Find each square root as a decimal.

10. $-\sqrt{0.16}$

11. $\sqrt{0.64}$

12. $\sqrt{0.09}$

13. $-\sqrt{0.0025}$

14. $-\sqrt{0.01}$

15. $\sqrt{0.81}$

16. $-\sqrt{0.0049}$

17. $\sqrt{0.04}$

Square roots and equations

To solve equations involving squared variables, simply get the squared variable by itself and use the square root to solve for its root.

1. Solve $x^2 = 25$

   $\sqrt{x^2} = \sqrt{25}$ Take square root of both sides of the equation.

   $x = \pm 5$ Solve for the roots of x. Write $\pm$ in front of the number to show that x can be +5 or -5.

2. Find the positive solution of $x^2 = 121$.

   $\sqrt{x^2} = \sqrt{121}$ Take square root of both sides of the equation.

   $x = 11$ Solve for the positive root of x.

3. Solve $x^2 + 8 = 72$

   $x^2 + 8 - 8 = 72 - 8$ Subtract 8 from both sides of the equation.

   $\sqrt{x^2} = \sqrt{64}$ Take square root of both sides of the equation.

   $x = \pm 8$ Solve for the roots of x.

---

1. Explain the steps to use to solve $x^2 + 9 = 73$ and solve for x.

Find the positive solution to each equation.

2. $x^2 = 121$

3. $x^2 - 52 = -3$

4. $x^2 = 625$

5. $x^2 + 19 = 119$

6. $x^2 - 10 = 15$

7. $x^2 + 95 = 99$

8. $x^2 + 14 = 95$

9. $x^2 - 25 = -16$

10. $x^2 - 25 = 144$

11. $x^2 - 50 = 350$

12. Write your own equation involving a square root. State the steps to solve and solve.

13. Explain how you would solve $\sqrt{x} = 6$ and solve.

Name _____   Date _____

The Pythagorean Theorem

A right triangle is a triangle that has a 90° angle. The sides of a right triangle that are adjacent to (next to) the right angle are called the legs. The side opposite of the right angle is the hypotenuse, which is always the longest side. The Pythagorean Theorem states that in a right triangle, the square of the length of the hypotenuse is equal to the sum of the squares of the lengths of the legs, written: $a^2 + b^2 = c^2$. Look at the triangle labeled to the right.

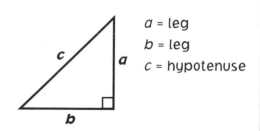

a = leg
b = leg
c = hypotenuse

The Pythagorean Theorem can be used to find the length of any side of a right triangle given the lengths of the other two sides.

    A right triangle has legs of lengths 6 and 8 inches. Find the length of the hypotenuse.

$a^2 + b^2 = c^2$	Write the Pythagorean Theorem.
$6^2 + 8^2 = c^2$	Plug in the values given.
$36 + 64 = c^2$	Square the numbers.
$\sqrt{100} = \sqrt{c^2}$	Take the square root of both sides of the equations.
$10 = c$	Solve for c.

Thus, the length of the hypotenuse is 10 inches.

note: The Pythagorean Theorem can be used to determine whether a triangle is a right triangle simply by plugging each of the values of the sides into $a^2 + b^2 = c^2$ and identifying if it creates a true statement.

1. Explain how to find the length of a leg of a right triangle if the length of the hypotenuse and the other leg is known.

In a right triangle, a and b are the lengths of the legs, and c is the length of the hypotenuse. Given each set of values below, find the missing value. Round to the nearest tenth.

2. $a = 15, b = 20$ 3. $a = 8, c = 16$ 4. $a = 18, b = 20$

5. $a = 2, b = 7$ 6. $b = 3, c = 7$ 7. $a = 91, c = 100$

8. $a = 20, c = 25$ 9. $b = 22, c = 30$ 10. $b = 11, c = 16$

11. The measurements of the sides of a triangle are 8 in., 9 in., and 10 in. Show that this triangle is not a right triangle. Give an example of the lengths of the sides of a triangle that would make the triangle a right triangle.

Name _____   Date _____

Using the Pythagorean Theorem   **Square Roots**

The Pythagorean Theorem can be used to solve many different types of real world problems. The first step to take when solving these problems is to draw a picture and label each of the sides of the triangle from the given information.

Looking at the picture below, find the distance from point A to point C.

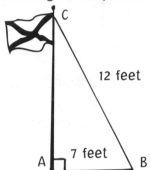

$a^2 + b^2 = c^2$	Use the Pythagorean Theorem.
$7^2 + b^2 = 12^2$	Plug in the given values.
$49 + b^2 = 144$	Square the numbers.
$49 - 49 + b^2 = 144 - 49$	Subtract 49 from both sides.
$\sqrt{b^2} = \sqrt{95}$	Take the square root of both sides.
$b = 9.7$	Solve for b. Round to the nearest tenth.

Thus, the distance from A to C is 9.7 feet.

note: When a perfect square is not given, use a calculator and round to the nearest tenth.

Write an equation that can be used to answer each question. Then solve the equation, rounding answers to the nearest tenth.

1. What is the distance from the ground to the place where the ladder touches the house?

25 ft.

6 ft.

2. How many miles apart are the two planes?

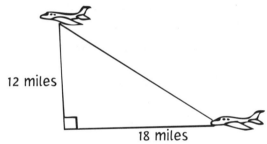

12 miles

18 miles

Solve each problem by first drawing a picture. Round answers to the nearest tenth.

3. Find the length of the diagonal of a square whose sides are each 8 inches.

4. John and Bob are 15 feet apart on the ground. If John is flying a kite and lets out 25 feet of string, and the kite is directly above Bob, how high is the kite?

5. On a regulation baseball field, there are 90 feet between the bases. How many feet are there from home plate to second base?

6. The width of a TV is 22 inches, and its diagonal is 32 inches. What is the height of the TV?

Square roots and formulas

Many formulas in mathematics involve squared variables. To solve these types of formulas, the square root must be found.

Use the formula $t = \sqrt{\left(\frac{d^3}{216}\right)}$, where t is the time and d is the diameter, to find the length of time a storm will last if its diameter is 15 miles.

$t = \sqrt{\left(\frac{d^3}{216}\right)}$	Write the formula.
$t = \sqrt{\left(\frac{15^3}{216}\right)}$	Plug in the given values.
$t = \sqrt{\left(\frac{3375}{216}\right)}$	Multiply 15 by itself three times.
$t = \sqrt{15.625}$	Divide.
$t = 3.95$	Find the square root and round to the nearest hundredth.

Thus, the storm will last 3.95 hours.

Round each answer below to the nearest hundredth. Use the formula $t = \sqrt{\left(\frac{d^3}{216}\right)}$ to find the length of time (t) each storm will last given its diameter (d).

1. $d = 20$ miles   2. $d = 32$ miles   3. $d = 14$ miles   4. $d = 18$ miles

Use the formula $A = \pi r^2$ to find the radius (r) of a circle with the given area (A). Use 3.14 for the value of π.

5. $A = 216$ in.^{2} 6. $A = 48$ cm^2 7. $A = 92$ mm^2 8. $A = 10$ ft.^{2}

Use the formula $d = \sqrt{8,000h}$ to find the distance (d) to the horizon given a plane's altitude (h).

9. $h = 0.75$ miles   10. $h = 0.5$ miles   11. $h = 0.25$ miles   12. $h = 1.25$ miles

Use the formula $V = \pi r^2 h$ to find the radius (r) of a cylinder with the given volume (V) and height (h). Use 3.14 for the value of π.

13. $V = 12,500$ cm^3, $h = 45$ cm   14. $V = 43,780$ mm^3, $h = 80$ mm

15. $V = 485$ in.^{3}, $h = 22$ in.   16. $V = 68$ ft.^{3}, $h = 18$ ft.

Review of Unit 9   **Square Roots**

Topics covered:

Square Roots	The Pythagorean Theorem
Approximate Square Roots	Using the Pythagorean Theorem
Square Roots and Rational Numbers	Square Roots and Formulas
Square Roots and Equations	

1. Give a definition of the square root of a number. Give an example.

2. Find two solutions to $x^2 = \sqrt{81}$.

3. Evaluate $\sqrt{49} - \sqrt{121}$.

4. Give the best integer estimate for $-\sqrt{75}$.

5. Explain how to find the square root of $\frac{9}{100}$ and find its square root.

6. Find the square root of -0.0036.

7. Explain the steps to use to solve $x^2 - 52 = -48$ and solve for its positive solution.

8. State the formula for the Pythagorean Theorem and explain.

9. In a right triangle, find the length of one of its legs if the other leg is 14 inches and its hypotenuse is 21 inches. Round to the nearest tenth.

10. Find the length of the diagonal of a rectangle whose sides are 38 cm and 26 cm. Round to the nearest tenth.

11. Use the formula $A = \pi r^2$ to find the radius (r) of a circle with an area of 210 in.^{2} Round to the nearest tenth.

12. Use the formula $t = \sqrt{\left(\frac{d^3}{216}\right)}$ to find the length of time (t) a storm will last if its diameter (d) is 7 miles. Round to the nearest tenth.

Unit 9 Test

1. Find two solutions to $y^2 = \sqrt{196}$.

2. Find the negative square root of 169.

3. Evaluate $-\sqrt{225} - (-\sqrt{400})$.

4. Is it possible to find the square root of a negative number? Explain why or why not.

5. Find the best integer estimate for $\sqrt{111}$.

6. Find the square root of $\frac{144}{49}$.

7. Find the square root of 0.81.

8. Find the positive solution to $x^2 - 91 = 30$.

9. Write your own equation involving a square root and state the steps to solve it and solve.

10. Explain if 12 in., 15 in., and 18 in. could be the lengths of the sides of a right triangle. Show using the Pythagorean Theorem.

11. Explain how to find the length of the hypotenuse of a right triangle if the length of the legs are 24 in. and 26 in. Find its length. Round to the nearest tenth.

12. Dan is cleaning out the gutters of his house. His ladder is placed on the ground 4 feet from the base of the house and is resting on the gutter. His ladder is 14 feet long. What is the distance from the base of the house to the point where Dan is cleaning the gutters? Round to the nearest tenth.

13. Use the formula $V = \pi r^2 h$ to find the radius (r) of a cylinder given the volume (v), 270 cm³, and height (h), 15 cm. Round to the nearest tenth.

Polynomials

A monomial is a number, a variable, or a product of a number and one or more variables. For example, -3, $3y$, $\sqrt{3}$, and $3xy$ are all monomials. Expressions that involve variables in the denominator of a fraction or variables with radical signs are not monomials. A polynomial is a monomial or the sum of two or more monomials. A polynomial with two terms is called a binomial, and a polynomial with three terms is called a trinomial.

1. $3x^2 + x - 12$ is a trinomial.
2. $4x + 1$ is a binomial.
3. $\sqrt{(5z)}$ is not a monomial.
4. $11 - (5/3a)$ is not a polynomial because $5/(3a)$ is not a monomial.

The degree of a monomial is the sum of the exponents of its variables. The degree of a polynomial is the degree of the term with the greatest degree.

1. Find the degree of $-5x^3y^4z$.

   $3 + 4 + 1$ Add the exponents.

   $= 8$

   Thus, the degree of this monomial is 8.

2. Find the degree of $x^2 + x^2y - y^4$.

   x has a degree of 2.   First, find the degree of each term.

   xy has a degree of 2 + 1 or 3.

   y has a degree of 4.   Greatest degree

   Thus, the degree of $x^2 + x^2y - y^4$ is 4.

note: It is easy to find the value of a polynomial if given the values of the variables involved. Simply plug these values into original polynomial and evaluate.

---

1. Explain whether $\frac{3x^2}{2y}$ is a monomial. If not, give an example that is a monomial.

Write **yes** or **no** to tell whether each expression is a polynomial. If it is, classify it as a **monomial, binomial,** or **trinomial.**

2. $-\frac{3}{4}x^2$

3. $-5x^2 + 6x + 7$

4. $\frac{x}{10}$

5. $3x - 10$

6. $\frac{7}{x} + y$

7. $a + b$

Find the degree of each polynomial.

8. $15x^2 + 6$

9. $x^4 + x^3y^2$

10. $-x^3y^2z^4$

11. $2x - 7$

12. $3x^5 + 9x^2 - 1$

13. $18x^2 + abc$

14. Evaluate $ab + cd^2$ if $a = -2$, $b = 4$, $c = 3$, $d = -5$.

Name _____   Date _____

Combining like terms

Using Algebra

A coefficient is the numerical part of a monomial. For example, the coefficient of $6x$ is 6. Like terms are monomials that are the same or only differ by their coefficients. For example, $8x$ and $-2x$ are like terms, as are $-3x^2y$ and $9x^2y$. To combine like terms, add or subtract the coefficients.

1. Simplify $3x + 7x - 8x$

   $(3 + 7 - 8)x$ Combine the coefficients using distributive property.

   $= 2x$ Simplify.

2. Simplify $3x - 7y + 8x - 12y$

   $(3 + 8)x + (-7 - 12)y$ Combine the coefficients of like terms.

   $= 11x - 19y$ Simplify.

Notice, in example 2, only like terms could be combined.

1. Describe the definition of a coefficient. Give an example.

Name the coefficient of x and y in each expression.

2. $3x + 5y$ **3.** $x - 10y$ **4.** $-7x - 6y$

5. $-2x + 9y$ **6.** $12x - y$ **7.** $4x + y$

Simplify each expression.

8. $7x + 5x$ **9.** $-18mn + 20\ mn + 5\ mn$

10. $-6x^2 - 8x^2$ **11.** $4x + 6y - 9x + 7y$

12. $-8y + 13y$ **13.** $-14ab + 2b + 9a - 5ab + a + b$

14. $2xy + 11xy - xy$ **15.** $6x^2 + 5x - y^2 + 8y - x^2 + x - y^2$

Find the perimeter of each rectangle.

16.

2.1x

1.5x

17.
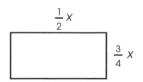

Solving problems using algebra

Many word problems in mathematics can be solved with one operation. However, problems are often translated into equations that involve more steps.

1. Brownies can be made with a box of mix and eggs. Twice as many eggs are used as mix. How many of each would be needed to make 15 batches?

   Let x = number of boxes of brownie mix.

   Then 2x = number of eggs.

$x + 2x = 15$	Set up the equation.
$\frac{3x}{3} = \frac{15}{3}$	Divide to get the variable by itself.
$x = 5$	Solve for x.
$2x = 10$	Solve 2x.

   Thus, 5 boxes of brownie mix and 10 eggs are needed.

2. Find the two consecutive integers that have a sum of -17.

   Let n = some integer.

   Let $n + 1$ = next integer.

$n + n + 1 = -17$	Set up the equation.
$2n + 1 = -17$	Combine like terms.
$2n + 1 - 1 = -17 - 1$	Subtract 1 from both sides of the equation.
$2n = -18$	Divide.
$n = -9$	Solve for n.
$n + 1 = -8$	Solve n + 1.

   Thus, one integer is -9 and the next integer is -8.

Write an equation for each problem. Then solve the problem.

1. A punch is made from lemonade and tea. Twice as much lemonade is used as tea. How much lemonade and tea is needed for 9 quarts of punch?

2. One number is 4 times another number and their sum is 20. Find the numbers.

3. The perimeter of a triangle is 26 centimeters. Two sides are the same length and the third side is 5 centimeters longer than each of the other two sides, find the length of each side.

4. The difference of two numbers is 12. One number is 3 times the other. Find the two numbers.

5. Harry paid $22 for 2 books. If one was $4 more than the other, find the cost of each book.

6. A rectangle is 20 feet longer than twice its width. If its perimeter is 520 feet, find the length and the width.

Multiplying monomials

A constant is a monomial that does not have a variable associated with it. The numerical coefficient of a monomial is a constant. To multiply monomials containing coefficients, or constants, follow these steps:

1. Arrange factors so the constants are together and the variables are together.
2. Multiply the constants.
3. Multiply like variables by adding their exponents.

For example,

1. Multiply $4x^3 \cdot 5x^4$

   $(4 \cdot 5) \cdot (x^3 \cdot x^4)$ Rearrange the factors to group the constants and variables.

   $= 20x^7$ Multiply the constants. Then multiply the variables.

2. Multiply $(-2x^3)(4x)(-6x^5)$

   $(-2)(4)(-6) \cdot (x^3 \cdot x \cdot x^5)$ Rearrange the factors.

   $= 48x^9$ Multiply the constants. Then multiply the variables.

3. Multiply $(-3x^4)(7x^6)(2y^2)$

   $(-3)(7)(2) \cdot x^4 \cdot x^6 \cdot y^2$ Rearrange the factors.

   $= -42x^{10}y^2$ Multiply the constants. Then multiply the variables.

1. Give a definition for a constant. Give an example.

2. Name the steps that would be used to multiply $-3x^2y$ and $6xy$, and multiply.

Multiply each expression.

3. $x^7 \cdot x^2$

4. $(8x^2)(-5y)$

5. $(2x)4$

6. $(x^4)(-7x)$

7. $(-3)(9x^2)$

8. $(\frac{1}{4}x)(8x^3)(-\frac{1}{2}x^2)$

9. $(-2x)(-2x)(-2x)$

10. $(-5x)(2x)(\frac{1}{2}x)$

11. Write your own expression multiplying three monomials. State the steps used to simplify it and simplify.

Powers of monomials

To find the power of a power, multiply the exponents.

Simplify $(x^2)^3$

$= x^{2 \cdot 3}$ Multiply the exponents.

$= x^6$ Simplify.

To find the power of a product, simply multiply the individual powers.

Simplify $(2xy)^4$

$= 2^4(x^4)(y^4)$ Multiply each variable's exponent by the power of 4 and take 2 times itself four times.

$= 16x^4y^4$ Simplify.

To find the power of a monomial, simply multiply each variable's exponent by the power.

Simplify $(x^2y^4z^3)^5$

$= (x^2)^5(y^4)^5(z^3)^5$ Multiply each variable's exponent by the power of 5.

$= x^{10}y^{20}z^{15}$ Simplify.

note: The same rules above can be used with negative exponents.

1. Is it true that $(-2x^2y^3)^3 = -2x^5y^6$? Explain why or why not.

Simplify each expression.

2. $(8^3)^2$

3. $-3(x^4y)^{-3}$

4. $(-2xy)^3$

5. $((-4)^2)^2$

6. $(-y^3)^4$

7. $(a^3)^{-7}$

8. $(-xy^2)^6$

9. $(4x^3y^4)^2$

Evaluate each expression for $x = -1$ and $y = 2$.

10. $2xy^3$

11. $-(xy^2)^3$

12. $(x^3y)^2$

13. $-4x^3y^2$

14. $-2x^2y$

15. $-(3xy^2)^2$

Multiplying polynomials by monomials Using Algebra

To multiply a polynomial by a monomial, the distributive property must be used to help in simplifying the problem.

1. Multiply $x^2(x + 4)$

   $x^2(x) + x^2(4)$ Distribute the x^2 to each term, x and 4.

   $x^3 + 4x^2$ Multiply each individual term by the monomial.

2. Multiply $-3y(5x^2 + 9y^3 - 2x^4y + 6)$

   $-3y(5x^2) + [-3y(9y^3)] - [-3y(2x^4y)] + [-3y(6)]$ Distribute $-3y$ to each term.

   $-15x^2y - 27y^4 + 6x^4y^2 - 18y$ Multiply each term by the monomial.

1. Explain how to find the product of x^2 and $x - 12$.

2. What property is used when finding the product of a monomial and a polynomial? Explain.

Find each product.

3. $8(3x - 5)$

4. $-5(4x^2 - 6x + 3)$

5. $2x(4x + 3)$

6. $6x(x^3 + 6x^2 - 7)$

7. $-3x(x^2 - x)$

8. $-x^2(x^3 - x^2 + 4x - 9)$

9. $-4x(9 - x^2)$

10. $-2x(6x^3 - 5x^2 + 7x - 10)$

11. $xy(xy + 10)$

12. $x^2y(-x^3 + x^2y + y^2 - x^2)$

13. Solve the following equation for x: $-3(2x - 12) - 3x = -45$.

14. Write your own equation involving a product of a monomial and a polynomial and state the steps you would use to solve it and solve.

Multiplying binomials

To multiply two binomials, multiply each term of the first by each term of the second by using the distributive property.

1. Multiply $(x + 2)(3x - 4)$

$x(3x - 4) + 2(3x - 4)$	Use the distributive property.
$3x^2 - 4x + 6x - 8$	Use the distributive property.
$3x^2 + (-4 + 6)x - 8$	Combine like terms.
$3x^2 + 2x - 8$	Simplify.

2. Multiply $(x + 5)(3x^2 + 6x)$

$x(3x^2 + 6x) + 5(3x^2 + 6x)$	Use the distributive property.
$3x^3 + 6x^2 + 15x^2 + 30x$	Use the distributive property.
$3x^3 + (6 + 15)x^2 + 30x$	Combine like terms.
$3x^3 + 21x^2 + 30x$	Simplify.

1. Explain how to multiply two binomials. Give an example.

Find each product.

2. $(x + 2)(x + 3)$

3. $(2x + 5)(x + 3)$

4. $(x + 6)(x + 4)$

5. $(5x - 2)(2x + 4)$

6. $(x - 7)(x + 5)$

7. $(x - 10)(x + 10)$

8. $(x + 8)(x - 9)$

9. $(x - 9)(x + 7)$

Find the area of each rectangle.

10.
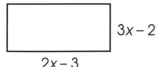
$3x - 2$
$2x - 3$

11.
$x + 8$
$x + 7$

12.
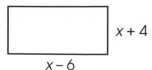
$x + 4$
$x - 6$

13.
$5x - 3$
$4x - 2$

Adding polynomials

To add polynomials, combine like terms. If it helps, first rearrange the terms so that like terms are next to each other.

Add $3x^2 + 9x - 10$ and $-7x^2 + 2x + 8$

$3x^2 - 7x^2 + 9x + 2x - 10 + 8$ Arrange like terms next to each other.

$(3 - 7)x^2 + (9 + 2)x - 10 + 8$ Combine like terms.

$-4x^2 + 11x - 2$ Add.

Another method to add polynomials is to arrange the like terms in columns and express the polynomial as a sum of monomials.

Add $-5x^2y - 7y + 12x$ and $9x^2y + 11y - 15x$

$\begin{array}{l} -5x^2y - 7y + 12x \\ + \ \ 9x^2y + 11y - 15x \\ \hline \ \ \ 4x^2y + 4y - 3x \end{array}$ Arrange like terms in columns.

Simplify by adding.

1. Name the like terms in $(x^2 - 7x + 5) + (3x^2 + 5x - 2)$.

2. Describe two different methods to find the sum of $(x^2 + 3) + (7x^2 - 6x + 2) + (-4x^2 - 2x + 5)$. Then find the sum.

Find each sum.

3. $(7x - 6x) + (3x + 8x)$

4. $(6x^2 - 8x - 12) + (4x^2 + 5x - 7)$

5. $(8x - 3y) + (4x + y)$

6. $(7x^2 + 16x - 11) + (6 - 9x - 9x^2)$

7. $(3x^2 + 6x) + (10 - 8x)$

8. $(x^3 - y^3) + (4x^3 + 3x^2y - y^2 + 3y^3)$

9. $(3x^2 - 10x + 6) + (6x^2 + 6x - 12)$

10. $(-7x^2 + 8y - 6) + (3x^2 - 10y + 9)$

11. Write your own expression involving the sum of three polynomials. Then explain the steps to simplify and simplify.

12. Find the sum of $(x^2 - 3xy + y^2) + (3x^2 - 2y - 5y^2)$ and then evaluate if $x = -3$ and $y = 4$.

Subtracting polynomials

To find the opposite of a polynomial, change the sign of each term of the polynomial.

Find the opposite of $-2x^2 - 5x + 8$.
The opposite is $2x^2 + 5x - 8$ by simply changing each term's sign.

To subtract a polynomial, simply add its opposite.

1. Subtract $(-6x^2 + 9x - 2) - (-3x^2 + 4x - 12)$

$(-6x^2 + 9x - 2) + (3x^2 - 4x + 12)$ Change each term's sign in the second polynomial and add.

$= (-6 + 3)x^2 + (9 - 4)x + (-2 + 12)$ Combine like terms.

$= -3x^2 + 5x + 10$ Simplify.

2. Subtract $(10y^2 - 3y + 1) - (4y^2 - y + 6)$

$$\begin{array}{r} 10y^2 - 3y + 1 \\ +\quad -4y^2 + y - 6 \\ \hline 6y^2 - 2y - 5 \end{array}$$

Change each term's sign in the second polynomial and add.

Simplify.

---

1. Describe the relationship between the addition and subtraction of polynomials.

2. Explain how to find the opposite of $(-4x^2 + 6x - 9)$.

3. Write your own polynomial. Add it to its opposite and find the sum.

Find each difference.

4. $(10x + 6) - (5x + 7)$

5. $(x^2 + 9x) - (4x^2 + 8)$

6. $(4x - 7) - (6x - 8)$

7. $(5x^2 + 8x - 12) - (3x^2 + 6x + 4)$

8. $(3x + 4y) - (x - y)$

9. $(7x^2 - 6x + 5) - (6x^2 + 3x - 11)$

10. $(10x - 5y) - (13x - 11y)$

11. $(6x^2 - 5xy) - (-7xy + 4y^2)$

12. $(6x^2 - 4) - (3x^2 - 9)$

13. $(11x^2 + 9) - (-7x^2 + 5x - 3)$

14. Find the difference of $(6x^2 + 9xy - 4y^2) - (3x^2 + xy - y^2)$. Then evaluate if $x = -1$ and $y = 2$.

Review of Unit 10

Topics covered:

Polynomials   Multiplying Polynomials by Monomials
Combining Like Terms   Multiplying Binomials
Solving Problems Using Algebra   Adding Polynomials
Multiplying Monomials   Subtracting Polynomials
Powers of Monomials

1. Explain what is meant by a monomial, binomial, and a trinomial. Give an example of each.

2. Explain whether $\frac{4x^2}{y}$ is a monomial.

3. Give the degree of $(x^2y^2 + x^2y^2z^2)$.

4. Name the coefficients after combining like terms in the expression
$(-12xy + 9y - 14x + 15xy - 7y + 12x)$.

5. One number is three times another number. Their difference is 32. Write an equation to solve for both numbers.

6. Multiply $(-2xy^2)(3x^3)(y^6)$.

7. Name the steps that would be used to simplify $-3(2x^3y^2)^3$ and simplify.

8. Explain how to find the product of x^2y and $7x^3 - xy + 6y^2 - 2x^2$ and find its product.

9. Multiply $(3x - 7)(x + 9)$.

10. Describe the two methods used to add polynomials. Then use each to add $4x^2 - 5$ and $-7x^2 + 6x - 3$.

11. Find the sum of $9xy + 10x - y$ and $-8xy - 2x + 5y$. Then evaluate if $x = 2$ and $y = -3$.

12. Name the opposite of $(-2x^2 + 9x - 4)$. What is the result when these two polynomials are added together?

13. Find the difference of $(-5x^2 + 2x - 7) - (-4x^2 + x + 2)$. Then evaluate if $x = 4$.

Unit 10 Test

1. Give a definition of a monomial. Give two examples.

2. State the difference between a binomial and a trinomial. Give an example of each.

3. What is meant by the degree of a polynomial? State the degree of $(xy^3 + z^3)$.

4. Simplify $(-3xy + 9xy + 5xy - xy)$. What is the coefficient of xy?

5. Jerry paid $48 for two shirts. If one was $12 more than the other, write an equation to find the cost of each shirt.

6. Name the steps that you would use to multiply $(\frac{1}{4}x^3)(2x)(-6xy)$ and multiply.

7. Simplify the expression $-2(x^5y^2)^4$.

8. Explain what property is used to find the product of xy and $9x^2y + 3x$. Then find its product.

9. Explain how to multiply two binomials. Give an example.

10. Find the area of a rectangle whose sides are $4x - 3$ and $x + 7$.

11. Name the like terms in $(-6x^2 + 9x - 1)$ and $(11x^2 - 7x + 4)$. Find the sum.

12. Add $(-3x + 10) + (5x^2 - 4x + 2) + (x - 6) + (-3x^2 + 1)$.

13. Write your own polynomial. Add its opposite and find the sum.

14. Find the difference of $(-12x^2 - 5x + 8) - (-8x^2 + 4x - 9)$.

15. Explain the relationship between addition and subtraction of polynomials.

Frequency tables

A frequency table is a great way to organize information. It is a table that shows how many times an answer was given.

Joe asked each of his 8 aunts and uncles how many kids they have. These were their answers: 4, 2, 3, 2, 4, 3, 3, 1

To better understand this set of numerical data, Joe needs to organize them.

First, Joe should find the range by finding the lowest answer and the highest answer. For instance, the range of his data is 1–4.

Now, Joe should make a frequency table to show how many times each answer was given.

number of kids	tally	number of aunts and uncles
1	/	1
2	//	2
3	///	3
4	//	2

note: This frequency table includes three columns: number of kids the aunts and uncles have, a tally (counts the number of times each answer occurred), and number of aunts and uncles having same number of children.

1. Give two situations when you might want to use a frequency table.

Find the range of each set of numbers.

2. 9, 8, 6, 9, 10, 9, 9, 8, 9, 8, 7

3. 6, 4, 1, 2, 4, 4, 5, 6, 1, 4, 1, 0, 0

4. 17, 19, 18, 15, 16, 19, 15, 16, 19, 15

5. 35, 32, 36, 32, 34, 33, 35, 32, 36, 32

6. Make a frequency table for each set of numbers in problems 2–5.

7. Create your own list of numbers for a specific situation. Make a frequency table for the set of numbers and identify the range.

Stem-and-leaf plots
Statistics and Probability

The stem-and-leaf plot is another way to organize a set of numbers. In a stem-and-leaf plot, the greatest place value common to all the numbers is usually used for the stems. The lower place value(s) form the leaves.

Make a stem-and-leaf plot for the following percentages:

92, 67, 85, 99, 82, 76, 73, 71, 89, 75, 62

1. Find the least and greatest percentage.
   The least is 62 and the greatest is 99.

2. Find the stems.

6
7
8
9

   The least percentage has a 6 in the tens place. The greatest percentage has a 9 in the tens place. Now, draw a vertical line and write the digits in the tens places from 6 to 9 to the left of the line.

3. Put the leaves on the plot. Record each of the percentages on the plot by pairing the units (ones) digit, or leaf, with its corresponding stem.

6	7 2
7	6 3 1 5
8	5 2 9
9	2 9

4. Rearrange the leaves so that they are displayed from least to greatest.

6	2 7
7	1 3 5 6
8	2 5 9
9	2 9

note: It is always nice to include an explanation of the data represented in the stem-and-leaf plots.

---

1. Name two situations in which you might want to use a stem-and-leaf plot to organize numbers.

Use the stem-and-leaf plot to the right to answer questions 2–5.

4	6, 8
5	2, 8, 9
6	1, 2, 5, 5
7	3, 4, 4

2. List the numbers in the stem.

3. How many numbers have stem 6?

4. Name the low and the high number.

5. What is the range?

Make a stem-and-leaf plot, using one-digit stems, given each set of data below. Then find the range.

6. 64, 76, 60, 96, 94, 58, 78, 54, 73, 78

7. 41, 15, 56, 38, 30, 19, 38, 23, 14, 40, 25

Counting principle

The possible number of outcomes can be found by multiplying. This counting principle states:

If event X can occur in x number of ways and is followed by event y that can occur in y number of ways, then the event X followed by event y can occur in $x \cdot y$ ways.

1. If there are 12 different flavors of ice cream and 6 different ways to get the ice cream served, how many different possible choices are there?

   Use the counting principle and multiply.

   # of flavors × # of ways = # of possible outcomes

   12 × 6 = 72

   Thus, there are 72 different possibilities.

2. If a die is rolled three times, how many outcomes are possible?

   # of outcomes the 1st roll × # of outcomes the 2nd roll × # of outcomes third roll

   6 × 6 × 6 = total # of possible outcomes

   Thus, the total possible number of outcomes is 216.

Find the number of possible outcomes given each set of information.

1. John tossed three coins.

2. A die is rolled twice.

3. The Jones family had 8 different poses to choose from and 4 different frames.

4. The Oriental Palace has a special on Tuesdays—pork, chicken, or beef, with steamed or fried rice, with egg roll, fried wonton, or crab rangoon.

5. Our company's uniform comes in navy, gray, or red in four sizes: small, medium, large, and extra large.

6. A coin is tossed, and two dice are rolled.

7. A new car comes with 2 or 4 doors, 6 or 8 cylinder engine, and 6 exterior colors with 4 interior colors.

8. Caroline has 8 silver necklaces, 6 silver bracelets, and 4 pairs of silver earrings.

Permutations

A permutation is an arrangement or listing in which order is important.

1. P(3, 2) represents the number of permutations of 3 things taken 2 at a time.

   P(3, 2) = 3 • 2 = 6

   Thus, the value of P(3, 2) is 6.

2. Find the value of P(9, 4).

   P(9, 4) represents the number of permutations of 9 things taken 4 at a time.

   P(9, 4) = 9 • 8 • 7 • 6 = 3,024

   Thus, the value of P(9, 4) is 3,024.

An expression written, $n!$, means n factorial, which is the product of all counting numbers beginning with n and counting backward to 1.

   5! = 5 • 4 • 3 • 2 • 1 = 120

Note: 0! has a value of 1.

1. Explain the meaning of P(5, 3).

2. Explain the difference between 5 • 4 • 3 and 5!.

Find each value.

3. P(6, 4)

4. 8!

5. P(7, 5)

6. 6!

7. P(4, 2)

8. $\dfrac{10!}{0!}$

9. P(5, 1)

10. $\dfrac{8!\ 4!}{5!\ 1!}$

11. P(8, 4)

12. $\dfrac{7!\ 6!}{6!\ 5!}$

13. Describe the meaning of 7!. Find its value.

14. Explain what the value of 0! is.

Probabilities

Suppose there are 15 marbles—9 red, 2 yellow, and 4 blue—all of the same size in the same bowl. Since only one marble is picked at a time, the two outcomes (picking a red marble and picking a blue marble) cannot happen at the same trial. Therefore, these are called mutually exclusive events. Use this information to answer these problems.

1. Find the probability (pr) of picking a red marble.

    pr (red) = # of red/total # of marbles

    = 9/15

2. Find the probability (pr) of picking a blue marble.

    pr (blue) = # of blue/total # of marbles

    = 4/15

Since these two events are mutually exclusive, the probability of either a red or a blue marble can be found by adding pr (red) and pr (blue).

Find the probability (pr) of picking either a red or a blue marble.

pr (red or blue) = pr (red) + pr (blue)

= 9/15 + 4/15

= 13/15

Thus, the probability of picking a red or a blue marble is 13/15.

1. What is meant by mutually exclusive events? Give an example.

Suppose there are 20 of the same size marbles in a bag—7 red, 8 yellow, and 5 green. One marble at a time is picked from the bag. Use the information to answer questions 2–8.

2. Name all possible outcomes.

3. Find pr (red).

4. Find pr (green).

5. Find pr (green or yellow).

6. Find pr (yellow or red).

7. Find pr (white).

8. Find pr (red) if all marbles in the bag were red.

9. Write your own example of a probability problem involving mutually exclusive events. Create four questions about this problem, providing the answers.

Multiplying probabilities

Independent events are outcomes that do not depend on each other. Each can happen independently of the others. For example, if a coin is tossed and a die is rolled, there are 2 x 6 = 12 outcomes. Tossing tails on a coin and rolling 5 dots on a die are independent events since they happen independently of each other.

Find the probability of tossing tails and rolling a 5.

pr (tails and 5)   = pr (tails) x pr (5)

= $\frac{1}{2}$ x $\frac{1}{6}$

= $\frac{1}{12}$

Find the probability of getting heads on a coin and rolling an even number on the die.

pr (heads and even #)   = pr (heads) x pr (even #)

= $\frac{1}{2}$ x $\frac{3}{6}$

= $\frac{3}{12}$ or $\frac{1}{4}$

1. What is meant by independent events? Give an example.

Suppose a quarter is tossed and a die is rolled. Use this information to answer questions 2–4.

2. Find the number of possible outcomes.

3. Find pr (heads and 4 dots).

4. Find pr (tails and an odd number).

Suppose a white die and a red die are rolled. Use this information to answer problems 5–9.

5. Find pr (white 2 and red 5).

6. Find pr (white 1 and red odd number).

7. Find pr (white odd number and red even number).

8. Find pr (white prime number and red multiple of 3).

9. Suppose the probability of you winning a car in contest 1 is $\frac{1}{100,000}$ and the probability of you winning a house in contest 2 is $\frac{1}{500,000}$.

Knowing these are two independent events, find the probability of you winning both the car and the house.

Review of Unit 11
Statistics and Probability

Topics covered:

Frequency Tables	Permutations
Stem-and-Leaf Plots	Probabilities
Counting Principle	Multiplying Probabilities

1. Give a definition of a frequency table. Give two examples of when it would be good to use one.

2. Find the range of the following set of numbers and then put them in a frequency table: 12, 10, 10, 9, 11, 12, 9, 11, 10.

3. Describe what makes the stems and leaves in a stem-and-leaf plot.

4. Make a stem-and-leaf plot using one-digit stems, and find the range of the following data: 45, 61, 53, 48, 75, 82, 63, 57, 72, 89, 87, 78.

5. Find the number of possible outcomes if 4 coins are tossed.

6. Find the number of possible outcomes if a shirt comes in red, navy, or white in a small, medium, large, or extra large.

7. Explain the meaning of P(6, 4). Find its value.

8. Describe the meaning of 5!. Find its value.

9. What are the values of 0! and 1!?

10. Evaluate $\frac{8!\ 6!}{5!\ 4!}$.

11. Suppose we are looking at 12 cars to buy—5 red, 3 blue, 4 black—and we can buy only one at a time. Find pr (black) and find pr (blue or red).

12. Suppose two dice and four coins are thrown. What is the probability of getting two threes and four heads?

Unit 11 Test

1. Explain the differences between a frequency table and a stem-and-leaf plot .

2. Identify the range in the following set of data: 1, 1, 5, 4, 4, 3, 5, 3, 1, 4, 3. Put the data in a frequency table.

3. Name two situations in which a stem-and-leaf plot would be a good way to organize information.

4. Use the following information to create a stem-and-leaf plot. List its range, the numbers in the stem, and the high and low numbers: 12, 39, 23, 19, 34, 45, 41, 31, 27, 11, 40.

5. Find the number of possible outcomes if a die is rolled three times.

6. Find the number of possibilities if a dinner offered mashed potatoes or baked potato, steak or chicken, peas or corn, bread or a roll, and cake or pie.

7. Explain the difference between $6 \cdot 5 \cdot 4$ and $6!$.

8. Evaluate $P(9, 2)$.

9. Evaluate $\frac{P(6, 3)}{5!}$.

10. Give the value of $\frac{2!}{0!}$.

11. Describe what is meant by mutually exclusive events. Give an example.

12. Suppose you have a deck of 52 cards—13 diamonds, 13 hearts, 13 spades, and 13 clubs, each containing cards 2–9, jack, queen, king, and ace. Find the pr (heart), pr (2), pr (king), pr (3 or 9), and pr (diamond ace).

13. Suppose a spinner has 6 equal regions—3 white, 2 red, and 1 yellow. Once the spinner is spun, a die is rolled. Find the pr (white and 4), pr (red and even number), pr (yellow and a multiple of 3), and pr (white and a prime number).

Answer Key

Page 5
1. ten; **2.** thousandth; **3.** meter; **4.** kilogram; **5.** liter; **6.** kilometer; **7.** centiliter; **8.** gram; **9.** millimeter; **10.** kilogram; **11.** centimeter; **12.** milligram; **13.** kiloliter

Page 6
1. addition; **2.** subtraction; **3.** multiplication; **4.** division; **5.** 15; **6.** 1; **7.** 49; **8.** 8; **9.** 3; **10.** 10; **11.** 4; **12.** 18; **13.** 56 ÷ (7 x 2); **14.** (12 + 8) ÷ 4

Page 7
1. 6; **2.** 6; **3.** 7; **4.** 5; **5.** 6; **6.** 2; **7.** 1; **8.** 3; **9.** 6; **10.** 34; **11.** 10; **12.** 8; **13.** 47; **14.** 39

Page 8
1. $n/9$ or $n \div 9$; **2.** $n - 5$; **3.** $n + 10$; **4.** $3n$; **5.** $2n$; **6.** $3n - 2$; **7.** $12 - n$; **8.** $5n + 4$; **9.–14.** Answers may vary. Suggested answers: **9.** the sum of a number and seven; **10.** a number divided by nine; **11.** thirteen minus a number; **12.** twice the sum of a number and four; **13.** eight times a number; **14.** four times a number, minus six

Page 9
1. An equation is a sentence that uses an equal sign. An inequality is a sentence that uses an inequality sign.; **2.** Fourteen is equal to eleven plus three.; **3.** Two times seven is less than fifteen.; **4.** Five times a number is less than thirty.; **5.** Twelve divided by four is equal to three.; **6.** A number minus three is greater than seven.; **7.** Seven is equal to seven.; **8.** $9 < 12$, $12 > 9$; **9.** $42 + 8 < 52$, $52 > 42 + 8$; **10.** $4 < 15 \div 3$, $15 \div 3 > 4$; **11.** $3 < 10$, $10 > 3$; **12.** $45 < 8(6)$, $8(6) > 45$; **13.** $40 - 12 < 38$, $38 > 40 - 12$; **14.** $5 + 4 < 18$, $18 > 5 + 4$; **15.** $14 - 5 < 10$, $10 > 14 - 5$; **16.** $16 + 14 < 15 + 18$, $15 + 18 > 16 + 14$

Page 10
1. 8; **2.** 56; **3.** 2; **4.** 42; **5.** 45; **6.** 5; **7.** 3; **8.** 5; **9.** 3; **10.** 48; **11.** 10; **12.** 9; **13.** 130; **14.** 8; **15.** Answers will vary. Two possible answers: $6 - x = 2$, $x + 3 = 7$

Page 11
1. 3; **2.** 2; **3.** 1; **4.** 0; **5.** 2; **6.** {0, 1, 2, 3}; **7.** {5, 6, 7, 8}; **8.** {2, 4, 6}; **9.** 2; **10.** 10

Page 12
1. 330; **2.** 300; **3.** 450; **4.** 1,800; **5.** 110; **6.** 37; **7.** 100; **8.** 72; **9.** 520 miles; **10.** $s = \ell - d$ where s = sales price; Answers will vary.

Page 13
1. adding 12; **2.** multiplying 7; **3.** dividing 4; **4.** losing 13 yards; **5.** subtracting 21; **6.** a withdrawal of $120; **7.** 23; **8.** 12; **9.** 33; **10.** 102; **11.** 135; **12.** 12; **13.** Answers will vary.; **14.** Answers will vary.; solution: $2

Page 14
1. km; **2.** Centi means hundredth., Hecto means hundred.; **3.** parentheses, division, multiplication, 12; **4.** 5; **5.** 13; **6.** $10n - 12$; **7.** three multiplied by the sum of a number and four; **8.** $45 + 10 < 60$, $60 > 45 + 10$; **9.** {6}; **10.** Answers will vary.; **11.** 60; **12.** subtraction, 70

Page 15
1. metric system; **2.–5.** Examples will vary.; **2.** 1,000; **3.** hundredth; **4.** 10; **5.** thousandth; **6.** Multiply and divide from left to right. Then add and subtract from left to right. 1; **7.** 14; **8.** Answers will vary. One solution: twice a number minus seven; Twice a number minus seven is greater than four.; **9.** $35 < 48 - 12$, $48 - 12 > 35$; **10.** 5; **11.** {0, 1, 2, 3} So 0, 1, 2, 3 are solutions.; **12.** 350 miles; **13.** Answers will vary.; **14.** division, 11; **15.** Answers will vary.

Page 16
1. 0; **2.** -3; **3.** 4; **4.** 6
5. ◄─┼─┼─┼─┼─┼─┼─┼─┼─┼─►
         -4   -2   0   2   4   6
6. 500; **7.** -10; **8.** -4; **9.** 12; **10.** 12; **11.** 0; **12.** 9; **13.** -10; **14.** 25; **15.** -15

Page 17
1. 300 miles south = -300; **2.** down 8 floors = -8; **3.** 10 seconds after liftoff = 10; **4.** $1,500 loss = -$1,500; **5.** 12, 12 feet backwards = -12; **6.** 175 feet below sea level = -175, 175; **7.** -35; **8.** 12; **9.** 70; **10.** 0; **11.** -128; **12.** -52; **13.** 0

Page 18
1. -4, -2, 1, 5
2. ◄─┼─┼─┼─┼─┼─┼─► $-1 < 3$
       -2   0   2 $3 > -1$
3. >; **4.** =; **5.** <; **6.** <; **7.** <; **8.** >; **9.** >; **10.** <; **11.** $4 < 6$; **12.** $35 > 15$; **13.** $23 < 41$

Page 19
1. positive; **2.** zero; **3.** positive; **4.** negative; **5.** negative; **6.** negative; **7.** 11; **8.** -5; **9.** 5; **10.** -23; **11.** -20; **12.** -20; **13.** $4,500 + (-$4,800), loss of $300 for two years

Page 20
1. 1 + (-3), negative; **2.** 10 + 5, positive; **3.** -8 + (-14), negative; **4.** -4 + (-7), negative; **5.** -2 + 12, positive; **6.** 20 + (-18), positive; **7.** -16; **8.** 21; **9.** -5; **10.** -9; **11.** 50; **12.** -20; **13.** -43; **14.** -7; **15.** To subtract an integer, add its opposite.

Page 21
1. positive; **2.** positive; **3.** zero; **4.** negative; **5.** negative; **6.** positive; **7.** -70; **8.** 32; **9.** 132; **10.** 0; **11.** 40; **12.** -80; **13.** -120; **14.** -39; **15.** 24, -30; If there's an even number of negative signs, product is positive. If there's an odd number of negative signs, product is negative.

Page 22
1. positive; **2.** negative; **3.** negative; **4.** zero; **5.** positive; **6.** positive; **7.** 11; **8.** 0; **9.** -5; **10.** -4; **11.** -3; **12.** 2; **13.** 6; **14.** 3; **15.** Answers will vary.

Page 23
1. subtraction; **2.** addition; **3.** subtraction; **4.** subtraction; **5.** addition; **6.** subtraction; **7.** 4; **8.** 100; **9.** 12; **10.** -1,000; **11.** 16; **12.** -28; **13.** -20; **14.** -6; **15.** Answers will vary.

Page 24
1.–2. Answers will vary. Possible answers: **1.** Multiply both sides by 5.; Answer is -35.; **2.** $9x = 27$; $x/3 = 1$; Answers will vary.; **3.** 7; **4.** -1; **5.** -12; **6.** -9; **7.** 4; **8.** 5; **9.** -120; **10.** 300; **11.** Answers will vary.

Page 25
1. $x > -4$; **2.** $x \le 4$; **3.** $x < 22$; **4.** $a < 11$; **5.** $r \le -24$; **6.** $n \ge 3$; **7.** $j \ge 12$; **8.** $e > 15$; **9.** $y > -20$; **10.** $-24 < x$;
11. $x \le 30$ ◄─┼─┼─┼─┼─┼─┼─►
                              0   5 10 15 20 25 30
12. $x > 150$ ◄─┼─┼─┼─┼─┼─┼─►
                              0 25 50 75 100 125 150

Page 26
1.–2. Answers will vary.; **3.** $y > 7$; **4.** $a \le 12$; **5.** $m \le -30$; **6.** $11 \le z$; **7.** $x \le -84$; **8.** $-18 > b$; **9.** $t < -9$; **10.** $x > 16$; **11.** -6; **12.** 55

Page 27
1. addition and division; **2.** multiplication and subtraction; **3.** subtraction and multiplication; **4.** subtraction and multiplication; **5.** subtraction and division; **6.** addition and multiplication; **7.** -18; **8.** 24; **9.** -12; **10.** -66; **11.** 11; **12.** -10; **13.** 7; **14.** 63; **15.** $4x - 3 = 5$

Page 28
1. <; **2.** ◄─┼─┼─┼─┼─┼─┼─┼─┼─►
                        -4   -2   0   2   4
-4, -2, 1, 3, 5; **3.** 13, Answers will vary.; **4.** 7; **5.** -25; **6.** -2; **7.** 5; **8.** -3; **9.** 7; **10.** -45; **11.** -10; **12.** $x = 36$; **13.** $b = -11$; **14.** $y < 3$; **15.** $h \ge -6$; **16.** $t = 20$; **17.** $c = -18$; **18.** $z \ge -9$; **19.** $k > -39$; **20.** $f = 41$, Multiply by 4, add 5.

Page 29
1.–2. Answers will vary.; **3.** 15 seconds after game time, -15, 15; **4.** 0, 0; **5.** 10; **6.** 28; **7.** -150; **8.** -19; **9.** -13; **10.** 24; **11.** Answers will vary.; **12.** $x = -24$; **13.** $b = -75$; **14.** $t \ge -34$; **15.** $x = 31$; **16.** $a = 8$; **17.** $a = 2$; **18.** $y < -9$; **19.** $18 \ge z$; **20.** $5x - 4 = 6$, Add 4, divide by 5 on both sides.

Page 30
1. no; **2.** no; **3.** no; **4.** yes; **5.** yes; **6.** $y + 6 = 12$; **7.** $17 + a = 21$; **8.** $4 + x = 12$; **9.** $15 \cdot h = 75$; **10.** $56 = 7 \cdot t$; **11.** $k + 11 = 32$; **12.** $3 = 8 + r$; **13.** $39 = f \cdot 13$

Page 31
1. (400 + 60) + 98; **2.** $3 \cdot (20 \cdot 5)$; **3.** $16 \cdot (25 \cdot 4)$; **4.** $(2 \cdot 5) \cdot 12$; **5.** 18 + (9 + 91); **6.** $(250 \cdot 4) = 1,000$; **7.** $(8 + 2) + 7 = 17$; **8.** $3 \cdot (-4 \cdot 250) = -3,000$; **9.** $(68 + 32) + 54 = 154$; **10.** $3 \cdot (25 \cdot 4) = 300$; **11.** $21 + (45 + 55) = 121$; **12.** $12 \cdot (5 \cdot 20) = 1,200$; **13.** $(75 + 25) + 19 = 119$; **14.** $(-20 \cdot 50) \cdot -29 = 2,900$; **15.** $(5 \cdot 10) \cdot 18 = 400$

Answer Key

16. $\frac{24}{4} = \frac{2(x)\,4}{4}$ $24 = (2x)4$

$\frac{6}{2} = \frac{2x}{2}$ $\frac{24}{8} = \frac{8x}{8}$

$3 = x$ $3 = x$

17. $13 + (6 + x) = 20$

$-13 + 13 + 6 + x = 20 - 13$

$6 + x = 7$

$6 - 6 + x = 7 - 6$

$x = 1$

$(13 + 6) + x = 20$

$19 + x = 20$

$19 - 19 + x = 20 - 19$

$x = 1$

Page 32
1. 5; **2.** 0; **3.** 17; **4.** 185; **5.** 32; **6.** 0; **7.** 33;
8. 18; **9.** 482; **10.** 26; **11.** 67; **12.** 0; **13.** 0;
14. 411; **15.** Answers will vary.

Page 33
1. 3; **2.** 3; **3.** 6; **4.** t; **5.** $4(12) + 4(15)$; **6.** $10t +$
$13t$; **7.** $r(7 + 8) + 2$; **8.** $3(a + 2b)$; **9.** $6x + 8x$;
10. $2(5x) + 2(8y)$; **11.** $8a + 15$; **12.** $10b + 8$;
13. $4k + 12$; **14.** $17c + 27$

Page 34
1. 1, 2, 4, 8; **2.** 1, 2, 3, 6, 9, 18; **3.** 1, 2, 4, 8,
16; **4.** 1, 2, 3, 4, 6, 8, 12, 24; **5.** 1, 2, 4, 7, 14,
28; **6.** 1, 5, 7, 35; **7.** no; **8.** yes; **9.** yes; **10.** yes;
11. no; **12.** no; **13.–19.** Answers will vary.
Possible answers: **13.** 4 x 9; **14.** 3 x 15; **15.** 3
x 6; **16.** 6 x 9; **17.** 13 x 2; **18.** 10 x 10

Page 35
1. C; **2.** C; **3.** P; **4.** C; **5.** P; **6.** P; **7.** C; **8.** C;
9. 2 x 2 x 2 x 2 x 3; **10.** 3 x 3 x 3; **11.** 2 x 2 x 3
x 3; **12.** 3 x 17; **13.** 3 x 3 x 5 x 5; **14.** 3 x 3 x 3
x 3; **15.** 2 x 2 x 2 x 2 x 3 x 3; **16.** 2 x 3 x 3 x 7;
17. Answers will vary.

Page 36
1. 7 squared; 7 = base, 2 = exponent;
2. a to the eighth power; a = base, 8 =
exponent; **3.** 9 to the third power, 9 = base, 3
= exponent; **4.** 3 to the sixth power; 3 = base,
6 = exponent; **5.** 12 to the fourth power; 12 =
base, 4 = exponent; **6.** x to the fifth power, x =
base, 5 = exponent; **7.** 9^4; **8.** 5^6; **9.** b^7; **10.** a^3;
11. 3×5^2; **12.** $3^2 \times 11$; **13.** $2^2 \times 37$; **14.** 2×3^3;
15. $9^2 = 81$, $10^2 = 100$

Page 37
1.–2. Answers will vary.; **3.** 4; **4.** 4; **5.** 11; **6.** 1;
7. 8; **8.** 32; **9.** 2; **10.** 1; **11.** 5; **12.** 20

Page 38
1. Answers will vary.; **2.** 30; **3.** 36; **4.** 175;
5. 60; **6.** 27; **7.** 150; **8.** 56; **9.** 60; **10.** 30;
11. 75; **12.** if the other numbers are factors of
the greatest number

Page 39
1.–2. Answers will vary.; **3.** 11^{13}; **4.** b^{13};
5. z^6y^2; **6.** x^{11}; **7.** 3^5; **8.** $-4x^5$; **9.** 4^7; **10.** 10^4;
11. $-20c^5d^4$; **12.** 8; **13.** 13; **14.** 9; **15.** 7

Page 40
1. $\frac{1}{4^2}$; **2.** $\frac{1}{7^3}$; **3.** $\frac{1}{b^{12}}$; **4.** $\frac{x}{y^5}$; **5.** $\frac{1}{x^7}$; **6.** $\frac{1}{5^{10}}$; **7.** $\frac{1}{15^4 f}$;

8. $\frac{3}{(ab)^6}$; **9.** 6^{-4}; **10.** 18^{-1}; **11.** $2 \cdot 4^{-3}$; **12.** cd^5;

13. b^{-1}; **14.** y^{-7}; **15.** xy^8; **16.** $2ab^{-3}$; **17.** $\frac{1}{a^4}$; **18.** $\frac{1}{c}$

Page 41
1. associative property—addition;
2. commutative property—multiplication;
3. identity property—multiplication;
4. commutative property—addition;
5. distributive property; **6.** distributive
property; **7.** identity property—addition;
8. associative property—multiplication;
9. 1, 2, 3, 4, 6, 8, 12, 16, 24, 48—Answers
will vary.; **10.** composite—$2^2 \times 23$; **11.** 12^4,
12 = base, 4 = exponent; **12.** 18; **13.** 72;
14. $\frac{1}{b^4}$; 15. $\frac{1}{a^3b^2}$, $a^{-3}b^{-2}$

Page 42
1. Answers will vary.; **2.** $b(8 + 9) + 24 = 17b +$
24; **3.** 1, 2, 3, 6, 9, 18, 27, 54, Answers will
vary.; **4.** Prime—factors are 1 and itself.
Composite—more than 2 factors, Examples
will vary.; **5.** $2^3 \times 3^2 \times 5$; **6.** 6^5, six to the fifth
power, base = 6, exponent = 5; **7.** GCF = 4,
LCM = 40; **8.** Answers will vary.; **9.** $\frac{1}{x^7}$, x^7;
10. 7^{25}, $\frac{1}{7^{25}}$; **11.** $\frac{1}{b}$, b^{-1}; **12.** $\frac{c^2}{d^2}$, $\frac{d^2}{c^2}$; **13.** $-3a^4$,
$\frac{-3}{a^4}$; **14.** $\frac{4m^5}{n^2}$, $\frac{4n^2}{m^5}$

Page 43
1. Numerator and denominator have no
common whole-number factor other than 1.
Examples will vary.; **2.** 5; **3.** 3; **4.** 12; **5.** 2;
6. 3; **7.** 11; **8.** 1/8; **9.** 11/18; **10.** 1/3; **11.** 2/5;
12. 5/8; **13.** 1/6; **14.** 6/7; **15.** 2/9; **16.** 2/5

Page 44
1. 9/56; **2.** 3/5; **3.** 5/12; **4.** 16/55; **5.** 3/65;
6. 13/49; **7.** 3/4; **8.** 9/20; **9.** 3/11; **10.** 25/81;
11. 1/10; **12.** 1/42; **13.** $4a/15$; **14.** 3/4 feet;
15. 7/36 yards

Page 45
1. 13/4; **2.** 41/6; **3.** 12/5; **4.** 7/4; **5.** 52/11;
6. 36/7; **7.** 17/2; **8.** 17/3; **9.** 1 2/3; **10.** 1 1/7;
11. 2 3/7; **12.** 1 7/9; **13.** 3 1/3; **14.** 5 1/5;
15. 2 8/11; **16.** 11 1/4; **17.** 2 1/10; **18.** 7 1/2

Page 46
1. 4/1, 11/2; **2.** 7/6, 8/7; **3.** 3/1, 47/9; **4.** 13/4,
16/5; **5.** 4/1, 19/4; **6.** 10/7, 41/10; **7.** 5/2, 7/3;
8. 25/4, 38/5; **9.** 10/3, 71/10; **10.** 10 1/2;
11. 4 1/8; **12.** 19 1/15; **13.** 3 3/5; **14.** 19 1/4;
15. 21 1/3; **16.** 10 5/8 in.²; **17.** 25 4/5 ft.²

Page 47
1. two numbers whose product when
multiplied is 1, Examples will vary.;
2. 7/4; **3.** 1/5; **4.** 10/3; **5.** 2; **6.** 1/16; **7.** 7/15;
8. 1 1/5; **9.** 6/7; **10.** 7 5/7; **11.** 20/33; **12.** 5/12;
13. 1 5/8; **14.** 7 1/3

Page 48
1. 1; **2.** 2 1/2; **3.** 4 1/2; **4.** 3; **5.** 9 1/2; **6.** 7 1/3;
7. 9 1/3; **8.** 12; **9.** 3 4/7; **10.** 2 1/2 miles;
11. 3 1/4 inches

Page 49
1. 8; **2.** 12; **3.** 16; **4.** 4; **5.** 20; **6.** 7; **7.** 16;
8. 30; **9.** 30; **10.** 18; **11.** 1 1/4; **12.** 5/16;
13. 9 3/20; **14.** 11/24; **15.** 2 51/56; **16.** 14 1/5

Page 50
1. 7 1/2; **2.** 5 1/7; **3.** 4; **4.** 4 2/3; **5.** 7 11/12;
6. 8; **7.** $x < 15$; **8.** $x \leq 4$ 1/2; **9.** $x > 4$ 3/8;
10. $x \geq 0$; **11.** $x \leq 11$; **12.** $x < 7$ 1/4;
13. Multiply by reciprocal or divide.;
14. Answers will vary.

Page 51
1. Numerator and denominator have no
common factor except 1.; **2.** 5, 2/7; **3.** 8/9,
replace 2 with 2/1, multiply 2 x 4, multiply 1 x
9; **4.** A mixed number is the sum of a whole
number and a fraction. An improper fraction is
a fraction whose numerator is greater than its
denominator.; **5.** 9 3/8; **6.** Change mixed
numbers to improper fractions. Invert divisor.
Multiply numerators and multiply
denominators. Simplify., 1/2; **7.** 15, 10 1/2;
8. Answers will vary.; Find the smallest
integer that each denominator will divide into
evenly.; **9.** 1 1/2, found 10 to be the LCD,
changed 2 4/5 to 2 8/10, changed each to
improper fractions with like denominators,
subtracted, simplified. Answers may vary.;
10. Divide by 3/5, multiply by 5/3, 15; **11.** 3
3/8; **12.** $x \leq 8$ 13/18; **13.** Answers will vary.

Page 52
1. 3, 3/7; **2.** Multiply numerators and multiply
denominators, then simplify the fraction.
Examples will vary.; **3.** Invert the divisor. Then
multiply numerators and multiply
denominators. Simplify. Examples will vary.;
4. Multiply the denominator by the whole
number. Add this to the numerator and put
this numerator over the denominator of the
original fraction. Examples will vary.; **5.** 1/4;
6. 11 1/5; **7.** 3 1/8; **8.** 2 1/28; **9.** 10 5/6,
Change 6 1/2 to improper fraction. Multiply
both sides of equation by 5/3. Simplify.
Explanations will vary.; **10.** Add or subtract
numerators. Keep the same denominator.
Simplify. Examples will vary.; **11.** Find the
least common denominator. Change to like
fractions. Add or subtract numerators. Keep
same denominators. Simplify. Examples will
vary.; **12.** Add numerators. Keep
denominators. Add whole numbers. Simplify.
11 3/4; **13.** Change to like fraction using 35
as LCD, subtract numerators. 6/35;
14. Subtract whole numbers. Subtract
numerators. Keep same denominator. 7 1/3;
15. Add whole numbers. Change fractions to
like fractions using 18 as LCD. Add
numerators. Keep same denominator.
Simplify. 16 1/8; **16.** Subtract 4 4/5 from each
side of the inequality. Divide both sides by 2/3
or multiply by 3/2. Simplify. Keep inequality. x
≤ 5 1/2; **17.** Answers will vary.

Answer Key

Page 53
1. three tenths, 3/10; **2.** five hundredths, 1/20; **3.** fifteen and eight tenths, 15 4/5; **4.** five and forty-five hundredths, 5 9/20; **5.** one and forty-seven hundredths, 1 47/100; **6.** eighty-one and fifty-nine hundredths, 81 59/100; **7.** one hundred twenty-five thousandths, 1/8; **8.** four hundred fifty-five thousandths, 91/200; **9.** 0.225; **10.** 7.09; **11.** 0.7; **12.** 7; **13.** 4.075; **14.** 41.8; **15.** 6/10, 0.6; **16.** 5 22/100, 5.22; **17.** 7 58/1000, 7.058; **18.** 8 85/100, 8.85; **19.** 615/1000, 0.615; **20.** 10 5/10, 10.5

Page 54
1. 5; 45,500; **2.** 4; 7.2; **3.** 5; 6,130; **4.** 2; 2,590; **5.** 8; 12.20 ; **6.** 6; 23.1; **7.** 3; 78; **8.** 8; 182.617; **9.** 685; 685.4; 685.37; 685.371; **10.** 0, 0.1; 0.09; 0.094; **11.** 1; 1.5; 1.49; 1.488

Page 55
1. Answers will vary.; **2.** to find an answer quickly when an exact answer is not necessary; to see if an answer is reasonable or not; **3.–14.** Answers will vary.; **3.** 64; **4.** 20,000; **5.** 2; **6.** 33; **7.** $5; **8.** 3,000; **9.** 23; **10.** $15; **11.** 400; **12.** 6,000; **13.** $600; **14.** 40,000

Page 56
1. Answers will vary.; **2.–11.** Answers will vary.; **2.** 140; **3.** 10; **4.** 8; **5.** 90,000; **6.** 3; **7.** 5; **8.** 3; **9.** 20; **10.** 4,500; **11.** 72; **12.** Answers will vary.

Page 57
1. Decimal points must be aligned.; **2.** none if decimal points are aligned; **3.** 9.75; **4.** 55.116; **5.** 0.5; **6.** 2.585; **7.** 19.28; **8.** 50.19; **9.** 9.27; **10.** 20.32

Page 58
1. Count total number of factors after decimal points. This is how many digits go after the decimal point in answer.; **2.** 8.2; **3.** 4.1; **4.** 5.75; **5.** 21.6; **6.** 2.5; **7.** 0.75; **8.** 141.4; **9.** 2.17; **10.** 0.036; **11.** 77.35; **12.** 16.81; **13.** 27.0756; **14.** $7.44

Page 59
1. 0.035; **2.** 42.4; **3.** 3.15; **4.** 2.252; **5.** 0.0053; **6.** 0.14068; **7.** 1.4; **8.** 0.43; **9.** 4.67; **10.** 4.1 gallons/hour; **11.** 16.1 miles/hour

Page 60
1. 92 ÷ 12; **2.** 1,600 ÷ 48; **3.** 14 ÷ 5; **4.** 108.1 ÷ 91; **5.** 8 ÷ 26; **6.** 2,475 ÷ 95; **7.** 32.5; **8.** 0.47; **9.** 2.56; **10.** 60.6; **11.** 3.2; **12.** 549; **13.** $1.24/gallon

Page 61
1. Divide both sides by 0.4., $x = 17$; **2.** Answers will vary.; **3.** $y \leq 0.5$; **4.** $d \leq 41.12$; **5.** $z = 17.28$; **6.** $t > 1.6$; **7.** $a = 0.3$; **8.** $z = 44.59$; **9.** $b \geq 2.743$; **10.** $x \geq 13.57$; **11.** $x = 1.226$; **12.** $c = 5.2$

Page 62
1. two and forty-eight hundredths, 2 12/25; **2.** 10 6/10, 10.6; **3.** 400, 351.3; **4.** 150—product; **5.** 500—sum; **6.** 6—quotient; **7.** $200—difference; **8.** Decimal points must be aligned.; **9.** Count digits after decimal points in both numbers. This is how many digits after decimal in product.; **10.** 19.98; **11.** 6.958; **12.** 9.92; **13.** 23.3; **14.** 1.212; **15.** 0.635; **16.** 53, Answers will vary.; **17.** $y \leq -11.73$

Page 63
1. 16/100, 0.16; **2.** 7 13/20; **3.** hundredths, 761.46; **4.** Find an approximate answer quickly if an exact number is not needed; find if an answer is reasonable.; **5.** 8 + 14 = 22; **6.** 25 ÷ 5 = 5; **7.** 400 + 100 + 800 = 1,300; **8.** 8,000 − 1,000 = 7,000; **9.** 10,000 x 13 = 13,000; **10.** 4,000 ÷ 2,000 = 2; **11.** Answers will vary.; **12.** 7.32, Steps will vary.; **13.** 16.696; **14.** 3.33703; **15.** 0.87; **16.** 14.22; **17.** 7,235; **18.** 45,921.7; **19.** $x = 19.82$; **20.** Answers will vary.

Page 64
1. right 4, up 2; **2.** right 7, up 10; **3.** right 2, up 2; **4.** right 3, up 0; **5.** right 3, up 11; **6.** right 0, up 5; **7.** (1, 2); **8.** (7, 6); **9.** (4, 1); **10.** (3, 4); **11.** (5, 5); **12.** (0, 0); **13.** See graph.

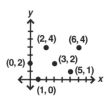

Page 65
1. right; **2.** down; **3.** right 3, down 2; **4.** right 7, up 6; **5.** no move right or left, down 3; **6.** left 1, up 4; **7.** left 4, down 5; **8.** right 7, no move up or down; **9.** (3, 3); **10.** (2, -5); **11.** (-6, 2); **12.** (-4, -3); **13.** (-2, 6); **14.** (5, -2); **15.** See graph.

Page 66
1. An equation is a linear equation if its graph is a straight line.; **2.** Find three solutions, locate points on a graph, and draw a line to connect the points.; **3.–8.** Answers will vary. Possible answers: **3.** (1, 3), (3, 9), (-1, -3), (0, 0); **4.** (1, -1), (10, -10), (0, 0), (-2, 2); **5.** (1, 5), (10, 14), (0, 4), (2, 6); **6.** (1, 12), (3, 20), (0, 8), (2, 16); **7.** (1, 1), (2, 0), (6, -4), (0, 2); **8.** (10, 5), (6, 1), (5, 0), (0, -5)

9.   **10.**

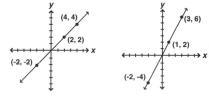

11.   **12.**

13.   **14.**

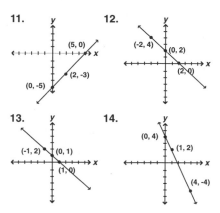

Page 67
1. Divide difference in y values by difference in x values.; **2.** From any point on the line, go down 2, to the right 1. This new point will be on the line.; **3.** 1; **4.** 2; **5.** -2; **6.** 3/2; **7.** -1/2; **8.** 0; **9.** -8/3; **10.** 7/4; **11.** Answers will vary but line will have same slant as line shown.

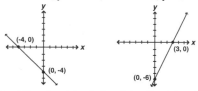

Page 68
1. Place points at (0, 2) and (4, 0). Draw a line connecting them.; **2.** Solve equations letting $x = 0$ for y-intercept, $y = 0$ for x-intercept. $x = 1$, $y = -2$; **3.** x-int = -1, y-int = 2; **4.** x-int = 3, y-int = 4; **5.** x-int = 1, y-int = -2; **6.** x-int = -4, y-int = -4; **7.** x-int = 3, y-int = -6;

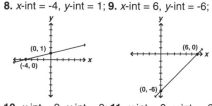

8. x-int = -4, y-int = 1; **9.** x-int = 6, y-int = -6;

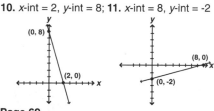

10. x-int = 2, y-int = 8; **11.** x-int = 8, y-int = -2

Page 69
1. Answers will vary.; **2.** (0, 2); **3.** (-1, 5); **4.** (1, 0); **5.** (2, 3); **6.** (-4, -1); **7.** (-2, 2); **8.** (0, 0); **9.** infinitely many; **10.** none; **11.** (5, 11)

Pre-Algebra

Answer Key

Page 70

1. $y > 7x + 2$; **2.** Test a point that makes the inequality true. Shade the region which contains that point.; **3.** solid; **4.** dashed; **5.** solid; **6.** yes; **7.** yes; **8.** no; **9.** no

10. **11.**

12. **13.**

14. **15.**

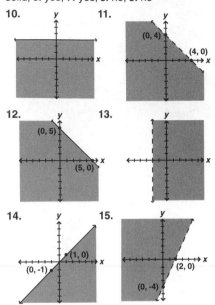

Page 71

1.

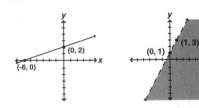

2. left 3, up 2; **3.** right 3, up 2; **4.** left 1, down 4; **5.** right 1, down 4; **6.** (2, 4); **7.** (-1, 2); **8.** (-3, -5); **9.** (4, -1); **10.** Answers will vary. See graph to right.; **11.** Subtract 9 and 1, 1 and -3, divide these differences., 2; **12.** x-int = -6, y-int = 2; See graph below.; **13.** the ordered pair that makes each sentence in the system true; Answers will vary.; **14.** (-1, 4);

12. **15.** No

Page 72

1. to the right; up; **2.** See graph to right.; **3.** A linear equation is an equation whose graph is a straight line. Examples will vary.; **4.** Solutions will vary. See graph below.; **5.** 3; **6.** Answers will vary. Lines should be parallel to line on graph below.; **7.** For x-int, let $y = 0$, solve for x. For y-int, let $x = 0$, solve for y. x-int = 6, y-int = 3; **8.** See graph below.; **9.** equations written together in the same problem; The solution is the ordered pair which is a solution to each of the equations.; **10.** same line, so infinitely many solutions; **11.** parallel lines; **12.** $y < -2x - 3$; **13.** No, because 1 > 16 is not true; **14.** See graph below. Only ordered pairs in shaded area is a solution. Answers will vary.

4. **6.**

8. **14.**

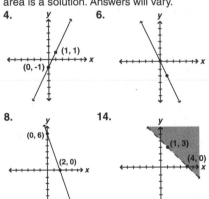

Page 73

1. A ratio is a comparison of two numbers with the same unit by division. Rate is a comparison of two measurements with different units. Examples will vary. $\frac{3\ cups}{4\ cups} = \frac{3}{4}$; $\frac{3\ cups}{\$5}$ **2.** Answers will vary.; **3.** 1/12; **4.** 7/9; **5.** 3/1; **6.** 8/1; **7.** 17 mi./gal.; **8.** 0.25 in./hr.; **9.** $0.68/lb.; **10.** $2.50/ticket

Page 74

1. 1/4, 2/8, 3/12, yes; **2.–7.** Answers will vary.; **8.** 1/5; **9.** 1/4; **10.** 2/3; **11.** 1/2; **12.** 5/3; **13.** 5/13

Page 75

1. A proportion is an equation with two ratios set equal. Examples will vary.; **2.** $x = 3$; extremes: 2, 30; means: 3, 20; Steps will vary; **3.** T; **4.** T; **5.** F; **6.** F; **7.** 12; **8.** 50; **9.** 36; **10.** 1; **11.** 9/27 = x/9.60, 3.2 gallons; **12.** 25/5 = 150/x, 30 boxes

Page 76

1. 220/4 = x/5, 275 calories; **2.** 8/6.40 = 12/x, $9.60; **3.** 1/15 = x/240, 16 packages; **4.** 7/2 = x/3,492, 12,222 votes; **5.** 325/5 = x/9, 585 miles; **6.** $\frac{1\frac{1}{2}}{60} = \frac{x}{36}$, 0.9 cups

Page 77

1. 60%; **2.** 55%; **3.** n%; **4.** 49%; **5.** 25%; **6.** 125%; **7.** 1/20, 0.05; **8.** 57/200, 0.285; **9.** 7/80, 0.0875; **10.** 3/2, 1.5; **11.** 3/5, 0.6; **12.** 5/8, 0.625; **13.** 12/25, 0.48; **14.** 3/1000, 0.003; **15.** 3/500, 0.006

Page 78

1. Move the decimal two places to the right and write the percent symbol. Examples will vary.; **2.** Set up the percent proportion and solve, placing the percent symbol after the solution. Examples will vary.; **3.** 32%; **4.** 12.5%; **5.** 33 1/3%; **6.** 16%; **7.** 350%; **8.** 147.5%; **9.** 60%; **10.** 308%; **11.** 7 1/4%; **12.** 200%; **13.** 120%; **14.** 66 2/3%; **15.** 50%; **16.** 83 1/3%; **17.** 150%

Page 79

1. 50%; **2.** 19%; **3.** 45; **4.** 20; **5.** 15; **6.** 84; **7.** 25%; **8.** 90; **9.** 38.88; **10.** 58%

Page 80

1. 15%; **2.** 35; **3.** 75%; **4.** $4,500; **5.** $36; **6.** $412.50

Page 81

1. D, 17%; **2.** I, 10%; **3.** I, 29%; **4.** D, 21%; **5.** I, 15%; **6.** I, 20%; **7.** D, 23%; **8.** D, 38%; **9.** Find the difference of the two. Then divide this by the original amount and change the solution to a percent. Answers will vary.; **10.** 37%

Page 82

1. Ratio is a comparison of two numbers with the same units by division. Rate is a comparison of two measurements with different units of measure. Examples will vary.; **2.** 8/17; **3.** 73.5 miles/hour; **4.** Answers will vary.; **5.** Set the product of the extremes equal to the product of the means and solve., 7.4, extremes: 7.4, 15; means: 3, 37; **6.** no; **7.** 720 miles; **8.** 75%; **9.** 34%; **10.** 420%; **11.** 197.5%; **12.** 13/40, 0.325; **13.** 33 1/3%; **14.** 60; **15.** 75; **16.** 29%, increase

Page 83

1. $9.45/15 lbs., $.63/lb.; **2.** 1/3, The ratios will vary.; **3.** A proportion means two equivalent ratios. Examples will vary.; **4.** extremes: 4, 12; means: 3, 16; yes; **5.** 15; **6.** 4/20 = x/55, 11 cups; **7.** Answers will vary. Decimal: move the decimal point to the right two places and add a percent symbol. Fraction: set the fraction equal to a number divided by 100; find the solution and add a percent symbol. Examples will vary.; **8.** 7%; **9.** 175%; **10.** 40%; **11.** 33 1/3%; ; **12.** 20%; **13.** 25%; **14.** 8/25, 0.32; **15.** 64%; **16.** 23.4; **17.** $780; **18.** Answers will vary.

Page 84

1. 8/13; **2.** 1/3; **3.** -2/9; **4.** -9/20; **5.** 5/12; **6.** 3/4; **7.** >; **8.** <; **9.** >; **10.** >; **11.** >; **12.** <; **13.** =; **14.** =; **15.** >; **16.** <

Answer Key

Page 85
1. positive; **2.** positive; **3.** positive; **4.** negative; **5.** negative; **6.** zero; **7.** -7.9; **8.** 8 3/4; **9.** -1/8; **10.** -1.2; **11.** 0.61; **12.** -1 5/8; **13.** -10 3/4; **14.** -6 1/2; **15.** $16.56

Page 86
1. -2.1; **2.** -14 2/3; **3.** -17.7; **4.** 7/16; **5.** -5/8; **6.** -1 3/14; **7.** -7/10; **8.** 0.9; **9.** -1 5/6; **10.** 1/9; **11.** A rational number is any number that can be named by a fraction with a numerator and a denominator that are integers. Answers will vary.; **12.** Answers will vary.

Page 87
1. positive; **2.** negative; **3.** negative; **4.** positive; **5.** positive; **6.** negative; **7.** -8.1; **8.** -30 2/5; **9.** 20/21; **10.** 18/25; **11.** -3.564; **12.** 1 1/3; **13.** 17.4; **14.** -58.88

Page 88
1. Flip the fraction equal to the number.; **2.** 0, 0/1 x 1/0 ≠ 1, A number cannot be divided by zero.; **3.** 1, -1 because 1/1 x 1/1 = 1 and -1/1 x 1/-1 = 1; **4.** 3; **5.** -1/4; **6.** -1/18; **7.** -10/63; **8.** -2/25; **9.** -1; **10.** 16/5; **11.** 2/11; **12.** 2; **13.** 0.4; **14.** 0.625; **15.** 12.5

Page 89
1. -6.7; **2.** -2/3; **3.** -13.95; **4.** -9; **5.** 2.7; **6.** -1 1/5; **7.** -1 2/3; **8.** -6; **9.** -21; **10.** 3/10; **11.** Answers will vary.; **12.** x/-2.3 = -8.5, 19.55

Page 90
1. -32; **2.** -49.14; **3.** -9/32; **4.** -1/10; **5.** -1; **6.** -28.5; **7.** -1.9375; **8.** -3/4; **9.** Add 4 to both sides of the equation. Then divide by 2/3 or multiply by 3/2 (both sides), 5 1/4; **10.** Answers will vary.

Page 91
1. The mean is the sum of the data divided by the number of pieces of data. The median is the number in the middle when the data is arranged in order. The mode is the number that appears the most in a set of data. Examples will vary.; **2.** 3, 6, 8, 9, 11, 21, 37; 13.6; 9; **3.** 9, 23, 25, 29, 31, 40, 46, 52, 64; 35.4; 31; **4.** 9, 12, 14, 16, 25, 46, 49, 58; 28.6; 20.5; **5.** 3.7, 4.2, 5.7, 7.1, 9.0; 5.9; 5.7; **6.** 85, 91, 101, 132, 151; 112; 101; **7.** 0.2, 0.5, 0.6, 0.9, 1.7, 9.2; 2.2; 0.75; **8.** Answers will vary.; **9.** 2

Page 92
1. Answers will vary.; 2.54 x 10^5; 5.3 x 10^{-5}; **2.** 6.784 x 10^6; **3.** -4.5 x 10^{-6}; 4. 8.9 x 10^{-3}; **5.** 9 x 10^7; **6.** -2.73 x 10^5; **7.** 1.7 x 10^{-12}; **8.** -32,000,000; **9.** 5,050; **10.** 760,000; **11.** -0.0008003; **12.** 0.000002389; **13.** -0.00000000432

Page 93
1. -13/14; **2.** the one with the greater numerator; **3.** sum: -0.85, difference: -5.97; **4.** product: -22.528, quotient: -2.2; **5.** numbers whose product is 1; Examples will vary.; **6.** 50; **7.** -2; **8.** -16.64; **9.** 49.2; **10.** -1 1/6; **11.** 8/27; **12.** -1/6; **13.** 20 3/4; **14.** -6.2; **15.** 11; **16.** Answers will vary.; **17.** 3; **18.** 7.64 x 10^6; **19.** 0.0000000906

Page 94
1. any number that can be named by a fraction with a numerator and a denominator that are integers; **2.** -3/5; **3.** -1/8; **4.** 5 1/4; **5.** -1/10; **6.** -40.92; **7.** 58/77; **8.** -11.02; **9.** Answers will vary.; **10.** 0; Explanations will vary.; **11.** 1 23/40; **12.** Subtract 4.2 from both sides of the equation. Then multiply each side by -3.9., 9.75; **13.** Mean is the sum of the data divided by the number of pieces of data. Median is the middle number when the data is arranged in order. Mode is the number used in the set of data the most number of times. Examples will vary.; **14.–15.** Explanations will vary. **14.** -4.15 x 10^{-7}; **15.** 7,980,000

Page 95
1. one of two equal factors; Examples will vary.; **2.** 2, -2; **3.** 8, -8; **4.** 3, -3; **5.** 7, -7; **6.** 1, -1; **7.** 10, -10; **8.** 12, -12; **9.** 20, -20; **10.** 5; **11.** -15; **12.** -9; **13.** 7; **14.** -6; **15.** -14; **16.** 11; **17.** 17; **18.** 22

Page 96
1. 10; **2.** 9; **3.** -8; **4.** 25; **5.** -12; **6.** -15; **7.** 3; **8.** -10; **9.** -11; **10.** 14; **11.** No, the square root of a negative number is not positive because two positives cannot equal a negative; not negative because two negatives multiplied together cannot equal a negative, not zero because the product of 0 x 0 is not negative, so a square root cannot be a real number.; **12.** Yes, if a negative number is squared, the result will be positive.

Page 97
1. Find the square root of the numerator and the square root of the denominator. Examples will vary.; **2.** 3/5; **3.** -4/6 = -2/3; **4.** 8/12 = 2/3; **5.** 13/15; **6.** 1/2; **7.** -7/11; **8.** -9/10; **9.** -5/7; **10.** -0.4; **11.** 0.8; **12.** 0.3; **13.** -0.05; **14.** -0.1; **15.** 0.9; **16.** -.07; **17.** 0.2

Page 98
1. Subtract 9 from both sides of the equation. Take the square root of both sides of the equation. Solve for the roots of x.; ±8; **2.** 11; **3.** 7; **4.** 25; **5.** 10; **6.** 5; **7.** 2; **8.** 9; **9.** 3; **10.** 13; **11.** 20; **12.** Answers will vary.; **13.** The opposite operation of $\sqrt{}$ is squaring. Square both sides of the equation.
$(\sqrt{x})^2 = (6)^2$, $x = 36$. Explanations will vary.

Page 99
1. Answers will vary.; **2.** 25; **3.** 13.9; **4.** 26.9; **5.** 7.3; **6.** 6.3; **7.** 41.5; **8.** 15; **9.** 20.4; **10.** 11.6; **11.** $8^2 + 9^2 \neq 10^2$, 64 + 81 ≠ 100, Examples will vary.

Page 100
1. 24.3 ft.; **2.** 21.6 miles; **3.** 11.3 inches; **4.** 20 feet; **5.** 127.3 feet; **6.** 23.2 inches

Page 101
1. 6.09 hours; **2.** 12.32 hours; **3.** 3.56 hours; **4.** 5.20 hours; **5.** 8.29 in.; **6.** 3.91 cm; **7.** 5.41 mm; **8.** 1.78 ft.; **9.** 77.46 miles; **10.** 63.25 miles; **11.** 44.72 miles; **12.** 100 miles; **13.** 9.41 cm; **14.** 13.20 mm; **15.** 2.65 in.; **16.** 1.10 ft.

Page 102
1. one of two equal factors; Examples will vary.; **2.** 9, -9; **3.** -4; **4.** -9; **5.** Take the square root of 9 and the square root of 100, write as a fraction, 3/10.; **6.** -0.06; **7.** Add 52 to each side of the equation. Take the square of each side, find the positive square root. Explanations will vary.; 2; **8.** $a^2 + b^2 = c^2$ where a and b are legs and c is the hypotenuse. In a right triangle, the sum of the squares of the legs equals the square of the length of the hypotenuse. Explanations will vary.; **9.** 15.7 inches; **10.** 46.0 cm; **11.** 8.2 in.; **12.** 1.3 hours

Page 103
1. 14, -14; **2.** -13; **3.** 5; **4.** No, a square root of a negative number cannot be negative because a negative times a negative is positive. The square root of a negative number cannot be negative because a positive times a positive is positive. Explanations may vary.; **5.** 11; **6.** 12/7, -1 5/7; **7.** 0.9; **8.** 11; **9.** Answers will vary.; **10.** No, $12^2 + 15^2 \neq 18^2$, 144 + 225 ≠ 324; **11.** Find the positive square root of the sum of 24^2 and 26^2; 35.4 in.; **12.** 13.4 ft.; **13.** 2.4 cm

Page 104
1. No, it has a variable in the denominator. Examples will vary.; **2.** yes, monomial; **3.** yes, trinomial; **4.** yes, monomial; **5.** yes, binomial; **6.** no; **7.** yes, binomial; **8.** 2; **9.** 5; **10.** 9; **11.** 1; **12.** 5; **13.** 3; **14.** 67

Page 105
1. numerical part of a monomial; Examples will vary.; **2.** 3, 5; **3.** 1, 10; **4.** -7, -6; **5.** -2, 9; **6.** 12, 1; **7.** 4, 1; **8.** 12x; **9.** 7mn; **10.** -14x^2; **11.** -5x + 13y; **12.** 5y; **13.** -19ab + 3b + 10a; **14.** 12xy; **15.** 5x^2 + 6x − 2y^2 + 8y; **16.** 7.2x; **17.** 2 1/2x

Page 106
1. lemonade = 2x, tea = x, 2x + x= 9; 6 quarts lemonade and 3 quarts tea; **2.** x + 4x = 20; 4, 16; **3.** x + x + (5 + x) = 26; 7 cm, 7 cm, 12 cm; **4.** 3x − x = 12; 18, 6; **5.** x + $4 + x = $22; $9, $13; **6.** 2(2$w$ + 20) + 2w = 520

Page 107
1. a monomial that does not have a variable associated with it; Examples will vary; **2.** Steps will vary.; -18x^3y^2; **3.** x^9; **4.** -40x^2y; **5.** 8x; **6.** -7x^5; **7.** -27x^2; **8.** -x^6; **9.** -8x^3; **10.** -5x^3; **11.** Answers will vary.

Answer Key

Page 108
1. no, $-8x^6y^9$; **2.** $8^6 = 262{,}144$; **3.** $-3x^{-12}y^{-3}$; **4.** $-8x^3y^3$; **5.** 256; **6.** y^{12}; **7.** a^{-21}; **8.** x^6y^{12}; **9.** $16x^6y^8$; **10.** -16; **11.** 64; **12.** 4; **13.** 16; **14.** -4; **15.** -144

Page 109
1. Answers will vary.; **2.** distributive property; **3.** $24x - 40$; **4.** $-20x^2 + 30x - 15$; **5.** $8x^2 + 6x$; **6.** $6x^4 + 36x^3 - 42x$; **7.** $-3x^3 + 3x^2$; **8.** $-x^5 + x^4 - 4x^3 + 9x^2$; **9.** $-36x + 4x^3$; **10.** $-12x^4 + 10x^3 - 14x^2 + 20x$; **11.** $x^2y^2 + 10xy$; **12.** $-x^5y + x^4y^2 + x^2y^3 - x^4y$; **13.** $x = 9$; **14.** Answers will vary.

Page 110
1. Answers will vary.; **2.** $x^2 + 5x + 6$; **3.** $2x^2 + 11x + 15$; **4.** $x^2 + 10x + 24$; **5.** $10x^2 + 16x - 8$; **6.** $x^2 - 2x - 35$; **7.** $x^2 - 100$; **8.** $x^2 - x - 72$; **9.** $x^2 - 2x - 63$; **10.** $6x^2 - 13x + 6$; **11.** $x^2 + 15x + 56$; **12.** $x^2 - 2x - 24$; **13.** $20x^2 - 22x + 6$

Page 111
1. x^2 and $3x^2$; $-7x$ and $5x$; 5 and -2; **2.** a. Combine like terms by rearranging them so that like terms are next to each other.; b. Arrange the like terms in columns and then express the polynomial as the sum of the monomials. $4x^2 + 8x + 10$; **3.** $12x$; **4.** $10x^2 - 3x - 19$; **5.** $12x - 2y$; **6.** $-2x^2 + 7x - 5$; **7.** $3x^2 - 2x + 10$; **8.** $5x^3 + 3x^2y + 2y^3 - y^2$; **9.** $9x^2 - 4x - 6$; **10.** $-4x^2 - 2y + 3$; **11.** Answers will vary.; **12.** $4x^2 - 3xy - 2y - 4y^2$; 0

Page 112
1.–2. Answers will vary.; **3.** Answers will vary; sum: 0; **4.** $5x - 1$; **5.** $-3x^2 + 9x - 8$; **6.** $-2x + 1$; **7.** $2x^2 + 2x - 16$; **8.** $2x + 5y$; **9.** $x^2 - 9x + 16$; **10.** $-3x + 6y$; **11.** $6x^2 + 2xy - 4y^2$; **12.** $3x^2 + 5$; **13.** $18x^2 - 5x + 12$; **14.** $3x^2 + 8xy - 3y^2$; -25

Page 113
1. Answers will vary. (polynomial: 1 term, binomial; 2 terms, trinomial: 3 terms); **2.** No, y, a variable, is in the denominator.; **3.** 6; **4.** $3xy + 2y - 2x$, 3 is the coefficient of xy, 2 is the coefficient of $2y$, -2 is the coefficient of x; **5.** $3x - x = 32$; 16, 48; **6.** $-6x^4y^8$; **7.** Find $(2)^3(x^3)^3$, $(y^2)^3$ to get $8x^9y^6$. Then multiply this by -3; $-24x^9y^6$; **8.** Multiply x^2y times each term of the polynomial; $7x^5y - x^3y^2 + 6x^2y^3 - 2x^4y$; **9.** $3x^2 + 20x - 63$; **10.** Answers will vary.
a. $(4x^2 - 7x^2) + 6x + (-5 - 3)$, $-3x^2 + 6x - 8$;
b.
$$\begin{array}{r} 4x^2 \qquad\quad - 5 \\ + \; -7x^2 + 6x - 3 \\ \hline -3x^2 + 6x - 8 \end{array}$$
11. $xy + 8x + 4y$, -2; **12.** $2x^2 - 9x + 4$; 0; **13.** $-x^2 + x - 9$; -21

Page 114
1. a number, a variable, or the product of a number and one or more variables. Examples will vary.; **2.** A binomial is a polynomial with 2 terms. A trinomial is a polynomial with 3 terms. Examples will vary.; **3.** the degree of the term with the greatest degree; 4; **4.** $10xy$; 10; **5.** $x + (x + 12) = 48$; $18, $30; **6.** Multiply $1/4 \cdot 2 \cdot -6$, x^3xx, y, $-3x^5y$; **7.** $-2x^{20}y^8$; **8.** distributive property; $9x^3y^2 + 3x^2y$; **9.** Multiply first two terms, outer two terms, inner two, last two. Combine like terms. Examples will vary.; **10.** $4x^2 + 25x - 21$; **11.** $-6x^2$ and $11x^2$, $9x$ and $-7x$, -1 and 4; $5x^2 + 2x + 3$; **12.** $2x^2 - 6x + 7$; **13.** Answers will vary.; 0; **14.** $-4x^2 - 9x + 17$; **15.** Subtraction of polynomials is the opposite of addition of polynomials. Change each side of second polynomial and combine like terms. Answers will vary.

Page 115
1. Answers will vary.; **2.** 6–10; **3.** 0–6; **4.** 15–19; **5.** 32–36; **6.** See tables below.; **7.** Answers will vary.

(2)
#	tally	frequency
6	I	1
7	I	1
8	III	3
9	₩	5
10	I	1

(3)
#	tally	frequency
0	II	2
1	III	3
2	I	1
3		0
4	IIII	4
5	I	1
6	II	2

(4)
#	tally	frequency
15	III	3
16	II	2
17	I	1
18	I	1
19	III	3

(5)
#	tally	frequency
32	IIII	4
33	I	1
34	I	1
35	II	2
36	II	2

Page 116
1. Answers will vary.; **2.** 4, 5, 6, 7; **3.** 4; **4.** 46, 74; **5.** 46–74;

6.
5	4 8
6	0 4
7	3 6 8 8
8	
9	4 6

range: 54–96

7.
1	4 5 9
2	3 5
3	0 8 8
4	0 1
5	6

range: 14–56

8.
5	26 26 26 41
6	15 34 76
7	08 27 41
8	10
9	09

range: 526–909

Page 117
1. 8; **2.** 36; **3.** 32; **4.** 18; **5.** 12; **6.** 72; **7.** 96; **8.** 192

Page 118
1. permutations of 5 things taken 3 at a time; **2.** $5 \cdot 4 \cdot 3 = 60$; $5! = 5 \cdot 4 \cdot 3 \cdot 2 \cdot 1 = 120$; Answers will vary.; **3.** 360; **4.** 40,320; **5.** 2,520; **6.** 720; **7.** 12; **8.** 2,520; **9.** 5; **10.** 8,064; **11.** 1,680; **12.** 42; **13.–14.** Explanations will vary.; **13.** $7 \cdot 6 \cdot 5 \cdot 4 \cdot 3 \cdot 2 \cdot 1$; 5,040; 7! means factorial; **14.** 0 factorial defined as a value of 1.

Page 119
1. two outcomes that cannot happen at the same trial; **2.** red or yellow or green; **3.** 7/20; **4.** 5/20 = 1/4; **5.** 13/20; **6.** 15/20 = 3/4; **7.** 0; **8.** 1; **9.** Answers will vary.

Page 120
1. outcomes that do not depend on the other; **2.** 12; **3.** 1/2 x 1/6 = 1/12; **4.** 1/2 x 3/6 = 1/4; **5.** 1/6 x 1/6 = 1/12; **6.** 1/6 x 3/6 = 3/36 = 1/12; **7.** 1/2 x 1/2 = 1/4; **8.** 3/6 x 2/6 = 6/36 = 1/6; **9.** 1/50,000,000,000

Page 121
1. a table that shows how many times an answer is given; Examples will vary.;

#	tally	frequency
9	II	2
10	III	3
11	II	2
12	II	2

2. 9–12;

3. The greatest place value common to all the numbers is usually used for the stems. The lower place value(s) form the leaves.;

4.
4	5 8
5	3 7
6	1 3
7	2 5 8
8	2 7 9

; range: 45–89

5. 16; **6.** 12; **7.** The number of ways 6 things can be picked 4 at a time; 360; **8.** 5 factorial means $5 \cdot 4 \cdot 3 \cdot 2 \cdot 1$; 120; **9.** both values are 1; **10.** 10,080; **11.** pr (black) = 4/12 = 1/3; pr (blue or red) = 8/12 = 2/3; **12.** 1/576

Page 122
1. Answers will vary.;
2. range: 1–5;

#	tally	frequency
1	III	3
2		0
3	III	3
4	III	3
5	II	2

3. Answers will vary.;
4. range: 11–45;
stem values: 1, 2, 3, 4;

1	1 2 9
2	3 7
3	1 4 9
4	0 1 5

5. 216; **6.** 32; **7.** $6 \cdot 5 \cdot 4 = 120$; 6! means 6 factorial or $6 \cdot 5 \cdot 4 \cdot 3 \cdot 2 \cdot 1 = 720$; **8.** 72; **9.** 1; **10.** 2; **11.** Answers will vary.; **12.** pr(heart) = 13/52 = 1/4; pr(2) = 4/52 = 1/13; pr(king) = 4/52 = 1/13; pr(3 or 9) = 8/52 = 2/13; pr(diamond ace) = 1/52; **13.** pr(white and 4) = 3/6 • 1/6 = 3/36 = 1/12; pr(red and even) = 2/6 • 3/6 = 6/36 = 1/6; pr(yellow and multiple of 3) = 1/6 • 2/6 = 2/36 = 1/18; pr(white and a prime number) = 3/6 • 3/6 = 9/36 = 1/4